Lemon Herbs

Lemon Herbs

How to Grow and Use 18 Great Plants

Ellen Spector Platt

Copyright © 2002 by Ellen Spector Platt

Published by
STACKPOLE BOOKS
5067 Ritter Rd.
Mechanicsburg, PA 17055
www.stackpolebooks.com

Printed in China

10 9 8 7 6 5 4 3 2 1

FIRST EDITION

Cover design by Wendy Reynolds
Cover photograph by Ellen Spector Platt
Interior photographs by Ellen Spector Platt, unless otherwise noted

Library of Congress Cataloging-in-Publication Data

Platt, Ellen Spector.
    Lemon herbs : how to grow and use 18 great plants / Ellen Spector Platt. – 1st ed.
      p.   cm.
    Includes bibliographical references (p.).
    ISBN 0–8117–2033–0
    1. Lemon herbs.   2. Nature craft.   I. Title.
SB351.L53 P63   2002
635'.7–dc21
                                             2001049024

For Annabelle Rose.
May you have a future filled with
lemon tarts and lemon squares
from Grandma's kitchen.

Contents

The Zest of Lemon Herbs

The taste of lemon enhances foods and drinks. A mist of lemon water cools the face. A rub of lemon cleans the hands. The fresh scent of lemon herbs infuses perfumes, bath oils, skin lotions, and scented candles.

I come by my preference for the taste and scent of lemon quite naturally. Lemon played an important role in my mother's cooking, where salt and pepper were kept to a minimum. In baking, it was either chocolate or lemon. She added lemon rather than vinegar to sweet-and-sour recipes. For a sore throat or cold, hot water with lemon juice and honey was the first remedy. It's no wonder that I favor the taste of lemon in my own cooking.

As I discovered the zest of various lemon-flavored and lemon-scented herbs, I broadened my repertoire. Lemon verbena and lemon geranium were my first lemon herbs beyond citrus, both prized for their scent in fresh or dried arrangements or potpourris as well as their flavor. I can never resist pinching or rubbing a leaf as I pass to increase the wafting fragrance.

Lemon thyme was the next important addition to my culinary repertoire. As a perennial it's easy to grow, and it packs so much flavor in those tiny green leaves, freezing hardly seems to diminish the zing.

Lemon grass started out in this country as an exotic herb associated with Asian cooking. It has become almost commonplace, and recipes abound in cooking columns and stems can be purchased in neighborhood supermarkets. I add minced fresh lemon grass to many dishes and have learned that favorite flavors don't need official recipes in order to shine.

Other lemon herbs like basil and eucalyptus, lemon bergamont and catmint give you twice the pleasure: a mingling of two delightful aromas or flavors to enhance the single more familiar note. They're fun to experiment with and to see how your own herbal supply can be expanded.

LEFT: *Ocimum basilicum* 'Sweet Dani'.

CHAPTER ONE

The Major Lemon Herbs

Some of the lemon-flavored and lemon-scented herbs listed here are well known and popular. Others are hard to find in gardens and catalogs but are well worth experimenting with. Annuals and perennials, shrubs, and even a tree are listed, along with some information on care, propagation, and uses. Be aware of horticultural zones for planting, and plan to winter over non-hardy varieties such as lemongrass, lemon trees, lemon verbena, and scented geraniums so you can enjoy them indoors while preserving them for the garden the next spring.

Plants are given Latin names. The first word, which is capitalized, is the genus, and the second word, which is lowercase, is the species. The species name is usually descriptive and may refer to the size, color, or shape of the leaf or flower, the type of flower, the growth habit of the plant, or the scent. In the case of lemon herbs, a distinguishing name of some of the plants, such as basil, thyme, catmint, eucalyptus, and monarda, is *citriodoro* or *citriodorus,* meaning lemon scented. *Citrinus* means citron colored or citronlike, *citrifolius* means citrus leaved, and *citratus* means citruslike.

Lemon Balm (Melissa)
Melissa officinalis

Lemon balm, sometimes shortened to just balm in old texts, is in the mint family, a bushy herb with small leaves scalloped at the edge. The leaves are bright green and leathery in the spring, forming a mound. Small, whitish,

LEFT: *Melissa officinalis.*

1

uninteresting flowers appear in late summer, and by that time the stems of this 2- to 3-foot plant are rather sprawling. Lemon balm is usually grown for its mild lemon scent and flavor, and not for its appearance, which is rather weedy. This perennial herb tends to spread. It is not as rampant as some mints, but it multiplies from dropped seed. It has the characteristic square stem of other mints and is very attractive to bees. In fact, the botanical name *Melissa* comes from the Greek word for bee. Lemon balm both attracts bees and calms them, and some beekeepers rub the hives and their hands with lemon balm when working with the bees.

Growing

Lemon balm is easy to grow in zones 5 to 9. It likes average soil, not exceedingly rich, in partial shade or full sun. In areas with intense heat, try growing it in partial afternoon shade or dappled sunlight. It grows very well in damp areas. In fact, I find it so vigorous that I use it in problem areas where little else will grow. Try it for preventing soil erosion on steep banks.

Start seeds indoors or in the garden, uncovered by soil. Don't allow to dry out. Or dig and divide by pulling apart established plants in spring or fall. Still another effective procedure is to take stem cuttings from the tips of a growing plant in the summer.

I often cut back the whole plant in midsummer, keeping the leaves to use fresh or freeze. Allow to grow a second crop for harvesting before frost.

Plant among roses, which often have bare canes at the bottom, or short-term perennials, to fill in the area with greenery. Cut off the flowers to prevent the herb from going to seed.

Culinary

Lemon balm is a favorite for multiple lemon uses, especially for teas and in cooking. Combine fresh leaves with pineapple sage in fruit salads and teas. Also use with black teas for a mild lemony, slightly minty flavor. Excellent in marinades for chicken and fish. Drying this herb causes rapid loss of flavor; use it fresh or frozen. Harvest leaves just before bloom for best scent and flavor.

Varieties

- *M. o.* 'Aurea' is somewhat shorter than the straight species, at 12 to 15 inches. It has golden yellow leaves but a similar taste and aroma.

- *M. o.* 'Variegata' has green leaves variegated with gold. It shows off its variegated color scheme best in moist semishade locations.

- *M. o.* 'All Gold' has leaves that are a bright chartreuse.

Lemon Basil
Ocimum basilicum

The lemon basils are annuals that need to be planted in full sun in well-drained, rich soil. Basil is native to southern Asia and Africa and hardy in zones 9 and 10. The plants have a compact bush habit, with spikes of white flowers. Its combination of lemon and basil flavors is a winner for culinary uses.

Growing

Grow lemon basil from seed or buy small plants from an herb grower in spring. Wait to plant till after all danger of frost. Avoid planting seeds indoors too early, as they are susceptible to damping off and to rotting in cold, wet soils. Seeds are easy to start directly in the garden, but up North, the growing season is somewhat short if sown in this way.

Lemon basil likes some moisture in the heat and will wilt if it gets too dry.

Keep nipping off the flower buds throughout the growing season for a nice, bushy habit and increased leaf production. Once you allow the plant to set seed, it will usually die. New plants may grow the next year from dropped seed, however, so after you've harvested enough leaves for the year, you may want to allow some seeds to form and drop.

Basil is very susceptible to frost, so be sure to complete your last harvest before the temperature drops to 31 degrees for even one night.

Basil is grown as a beloved kitchen herb and as such belongs as close to the kitchen door as possible. If you plant it too many steps away, when you're rushed or just plain lazy, you'll pass up nipping off those few crucial leaves you need to make your culinary efforts sing and resort to some old dried stuff you've had for too many years in your spice rack.

Culinary

Use lemon basil in teas, salads, and cooking, replacing regular basil in any recipe, including your favorite pesto. Lemon basil can fully flavor an herbal vinegar, oil, or salad dressing without a lot of other additions.

Lemon Basil. *Ocimum basilicum* 'Mrs. Burns'.

Varieties

- *Ocimum americanum.*

- *Ocimum citriodorum,* a small, pointed-leafed variety, grows to 15 inches.

- *Ocimum basilicum* 'Mrs. Burns', a tall grower at 24 inches, has bright green leaves, and 'Sweet Dani', an All-American Selection award winner, has larger leaves and is slower to bolt than other varieties.

Lemon Monarda, Bergamot, or Bee Balm
Monarda citriodora

This charming plant has lavender flowers growing in whorls up a bare, square stem. This plant is sometimes called lemon mint, but don't confuse it with the *Mentha.* Always buy plants or seeds by botanical name so you get what you want. Lemon monarda is native to the Southwest.

Growing

Lemon monarda is easy to start from seed either indoors or in the garden. Plant this annual in full sun. It can use some moisture and partial shade, but as the monardas are susceptible to powdery mildew, they need good air circulation, with no overhead watering. Lemon monarda can withstand high heat if dry and not humid. If you don't cut it all for vases or for drying, it will self-seed.

Beautiful in combination with other colorful annuals, filling in spaces in a perennial bed or in a traditional herb garden. Flowers attract bees, butterflies, and hummingbirds. It's one of the few lemon-scented herbs with showy flowers.

Culinary

Use young leaves in teas and to flavor salads and stuffings. This herb was used by the Hopi Indians to flavor game and to make a tea.

Lemon Catmint
Nepeta cataria 'Citriodora'

A perennial catmint with a lemon fragrance, it has green-gray downy foliage and grows to 2 feet in full sun or partial shade in zones 3 to 9. This member of the mint family has white flowers with lavender spots. Cats may like this as well as the regular species, but if you're a cat owner, you know how independent and finicky they can be, so there are no guarantees on this one.

Monarda citriodora, with zinnia 'Pink Splendor' and verbena 'Homestead Purple'.

Catmint is native to Southeast Asia and Europe and was brought to the United States by settlers. It has since escaped into the wild and is found in many areas of the country.

Growing

This plant grows easily from division or from cuttings in spring to midsummer. It is rather sprawling and weedy looking, not an especially attractive garden plant. Likes moist soil but tolerates dryness.

It attracts many cats, especially female, but not only your pets. Larger cats, such as bobcats, cougars, lynx, and mountain lions, have been trapped in the wild with lures of catmint.

Citronella Grass
Cymbopogon nardus

The oil from this plant is used as an insect repellent and to scent candles and incense sticks. It may also repel cats. It is also sometimes used in cooking but is not as highly thought of for culinary use as lemongrass, a favorite in Thai and other Asian cuisines. Citronella grass is used in cheaper cosmetics. It is a tender perennial that grows up to 6 feet tall.

Nepeta cataria 'Citriodora'.

Lemon Eucalyptus (Lemon Gum Tree)
Eucalyptus citriodora

Lance-shaped leaves of this tree smell of lemon when crushed. In tropical zones, it may grow 80 to 160 feet tall and 50 to 100 feet wide. It shows white flowers in summer. In more moderate climates, gardeners treat it tenderly, growing it in a tub as a houseplant. Plant in containers to enjoy on the patio and bring indoors for the winter. Hardy in zones 9 to 10. This hard-to-find plant is available by mail from Sandy Mush Herb Nursery (see Sources).

Eucalyptus citriodora.

Lemon-Scented Geranium
Pelargonium

These plants are in a different family from true geraniums, but everyone calls them scented geraniums. They are native to South Africa, where there are over six hundred species growing wild. In their native habitat, some are shrubby, reaching 10 feet high, and are true perennials. They were brought to England in the late 1600s and to New Zealand. Their showy cousins are extremely popular for window boxes and bedding plants. The scented geraniums are not frost hardy. North of zone 9, they are usually grown as annuals or houseplants.

The scented geraniums are a family of much-loved plants grown for the scent in their leaves, not for the usually insignificant flowers. The simple flowers have five petals, four to ten flowers per stem. Some gardeners treat them as houseplants and never set them out in the garden, but most move these plants in and out with the change of seasons. Where the flowers are attractive, count this as a bonus to the fantastic fragrance. Especially if the plant is moved in and out, the flowers may not bloom at all.

Growing

The plants are easy to grow from cuttings and readily set seed and cross-pollinate. Growers have fun coming up with new varieties, seeking changes of scent, flower color, and leaf shape, size, and color. The rose-scented geraniums are probably the most popular, followed by the lemon scented, but those with apple, coconut, almond, chocolate peppermint, nutmeg, and filbert scents are also appealing.

Grow as an annual or as a houseplant with lots of sun. Lemon geraniums need good air circulation, so don't stuff them in too closely next to other plants. Provide excellent drainage in a somewhat sandy soil, and don't allow to stand in water where the roots can rot. Grow as a standard, in a hanging basket, or in pots on the patio. Water when dry to the touch. If grown outdoors in a pot, it's easy to bring the plant indoors in the winter. Beware of whitefly. Wash all surfaces of leaves carefully before bringing indoors.

Culinary

Lemon geranium leaves are used most frequently in desserts, jellies, other sweet dishes like fruit salads, and teas. Because of the decorative shape of the leaves, they are sometimes embedded in the surface of pound cakes and sugar cookies both to impart flavor and for embellishment.

Rub lemon geranium leaves on wood to enhance the shine and perfume the room. This variety is 'Rober's Lemon Rose'.

Varieties

- *Pelargonium × asperum* 'Lemon Mabel' has a light fragrance.

- *P. cucullatum* 'Spanish Lavender' has large leaves, 2 to 3 inches, a pungent aroma, and flowers of intense purple.

- *P. citronellum* 'Mabel Grey' is a tall plant with a strong bitter lemon scent, dark green deeply lobed leaves, and pink and purple flowers. Good for training into a standard.

- *P. crispum,* also called 'Finger Bowl' geranium, has small, 1/2-inch crinkled leaves, a dwarf, upright habit, and lavender-pink flowers.

- *P. c.* 'Prince Rupert' leaves are larger than those of *P. crispum,* at 1/2 to 11/2 inches. Can be trained well for standards.

- *P. c.* 'Prince Rupert Variegata' is a compact plant with pink flowers and variegated cream and white leaves. Also known as 'French Lace'.

- *P. c.* 'Large Flowered Crispum' has large petals.

Pelargonium crispum 'Prince Rupert'.

- *P. c.* 'Variegatum Aureum Well-Sweep' has pink flowers and golden green leaves.

- *P. mellissinum* 'Lemon Balm' is tall with coarse leaves, lavender-pink flowers, and vigorous, upright growth.

- *P.* 'Bitter Lemon' has a strong lemon scent, pale lavender flowers, and deeply lobed leaves.

- *P.* 'Frensham', similar to 'Bitter Lemon', is a sturdy hybrid of 'Mabel Grey' but with smaller leaves. One of the best for flowering, pink and mauve.

Pelargonium graveolens 'Rober's Lemon Rose' with Lemon Verbena.

- *P. graveolens* 'Rober's Lemon Rose' has scalloped, fuzzy, gray-green leaves, and pale pink flowers. My personal favorite, combining two beloved scents and flavors.

- *P. domesticum* × lemon-scented *pelargonium* 'Roger's Delight' has deeply lobed leaves with strong scent and showy pink flower with maroon center. Good for hanging baskets.

- *P. vitifolium* is a large plant with bright green leaves and a lemon-rose scent.

Lemongrass
Cymbopogon flexuosus (East Indian lemongrass)
Cymbopogon citratus (West Indian lemongrass)

Lush grasses with tall, narrow, 1- to 2-inch-wide green leaves with a bluish cast. Grow as a landscape grass, but especially for the characteristic sweet, lemony perfume and flavor. In frost-free areas, a clump will grow up to 6 feet tall.

Growing

Buy small plants from herb farms and catalogs or start from seed. (See Territorial Seed Company in Sources.) Lemongrass can also be grown from root cuttings. You may be able to do this from fresh stems of lemongrass you purchase in an Asian or specialty market. The stem must have little pieces of root buds attached. Trim the top to 5 inches tall, and pot up in a light potting mixture, keeping the soil moist and the plant in a sunny area. When the roots are established, plant outdoors in the garden or in a planter on the patio.

Grow lemongrass as a tender perennial. It will grow 2 to 3 feet tall in areas with winter frost. Bring pots indoors to winter over. If you grow this lovely, delicious grass as an annual or an indoor plant, expect no blooms; be pleasantly surprised if you get any. In more tropical climates, lemongrass will produce many stems of flowering panicles.

In pots, water freely in summer, but cut back a little when you bring the plant indoors in autumn. Likes a light, fertile, well-drained soil with full sun.

Grow as part of a grassy border or mixed with other plants. The tan leaves are lovely in the winter, and even though the plants in my zone 5.5 garden must be discarded in spring, I leave them to rustle and sway in the winter winds so that I can enjoy their parchment color, texture, and form along with their tunes.

Culinary

Useful in Thai, Vietnamese, and other Asian recipes, including soups, meat dishes, teas, and desserts. The base of each stem of *C. citratus* is fleshy, something like a scallion. The heart of this lower stem is the part prized for use in cooking. It will keep in the refrigerator for a month or more, but fresher is always more flavorful.

Make a lemongrass syrup useful in many fruit desserts and fruit ades. Chop 3 cups lower leaves and stalks roughly in a food processor. Boil with 3 cups water and 3 cups sugar until reduced by about half. Strain and store in glass jar in the refrigerator. Add to fruit salads, poached fresh summer peaches or plums, iced teas, and fruit ades of any flavor.

Mexican Giant Hyssop
Agastache mexicana

This 5-foot-tall perennial hyssop has lemon-scented foliage and edible reddish purple flowers on long spikes in mid to late summer. Grow as an annual in colder climates by starting early indoors. Hardy in zones 7 to 11.

Lemon Mint
Mentha × *piperita* var. *citrata*

A perennial lemon-flavored mint with pale green leaves, growing 1 to 2 feet tall. Like other mints, it is aggressive and invasive but can be an excellent ground cover. Use caution as to where you plant this. Lavender flowers are not showy. It's parents are the apple mint and lime mint with a spearmint flavor. Don't confuse with another plant sometimes called lemon mint, the lemon monarda (also called bee balm or bergamot), which is related but looks and tastes very different.

Growing

Propagate from division of a known plant or from cuttings, as seeds are not always true to type. In fact, mints hybridize almost too easily, and plants are often mislabeled at the garden center. Anyone who has the mint will be only too happy to share cuttings or divisions.

Plant in full or partial sun. Grow mints in a container to control spreading, or plant in an area where spreading is acceptable or desirable.

Mentha × *piperita* var. *citrata*.

Culinary

The combination of lemon and mint flavors makes it a natural for tea or with fish, chicken, or lamb.

Freeze sprigs of lemon mint in ice cube trays with water. Use the cubes to flavor cool summer drinks.

Variety

- *Mentha* 'Hillary's Sweet Lemon', named for Hillary Clinton, has lavender flower spikes.

Marigold 'Lemon Gem'
Tagetes tenuifolia

A small, showy, single-flowered marigold with a pungent lemon flavor and aroma. An annual that is an excellent addition to any herb garden for its cheery color and bushy habit. It has a 1-by-1-foot spread. The plant is completely covered with small, single flowers and has finely cut, fernlike leaves.

Tagetes tenuifolia.

Growing

Plant in full sun. Very easy to grow from seed started indoors or in the garden. Useful as a bedding or edging plant in the front of the border. Excellent in any herb garden, as well as those with a lemon theme, because of its rich color and mounded habit, blooming until hit by a heavy frost. Also strew plants throughout the garden for possible control of nematodes and other insects.

Culinary

This marigold flower is edible. Mix petals in salads or float in teas for decorative effect. Richters Seed Company recommends use in warm dessert sauces made with wine. A raspberry sauce made with white wine and a few floating 'Lemon Gem' marigolds poured over a fine-quality vanilla ice cream would make an exotic but easy dessert.

Pepper 'Lemon Drop'

A small, yellow hot pepper in the habañero family, with a distinct citrus flavor. I've never seen seeds sold commercially for this variety. Grower Jim Weaver of Meadow View Farm (see Sources) says he got the seeds originally from the U.S.

Use 'Lemon Drop' peppers for color and heat in herbal vinegars.

Dept. of Agriculture in a batch of heirloom varieties of seeds. He saves the seeds each year to replant, as it's one of his two most popular peppers out of the 175 varieties he grows. He uses it for hot pepper jelly, hot sauces, and the like.

Lemon Santolina
Santolina ericoides

A perennial plant for the border or rock garden, with a sweet button-type flower and a fresh, clean scent. Grows to 12 inches in a neat, compact shrub. Lovely for the front of the border, to edge an herb bed, or in a rockery. The flower air-dries well.

Lemon Savory
Satureja biflora

Grow as a tender perennial, since its native habitat is South Africa. It displays small white or lilac flowers. Likes full sun but tolerates partial shade. The strong lemon flavor and scent are used in cooking and in teas. Savory generally has a spicy smell and a spicy and peppery taste and, as the name implies, is used in savory dishes.

Sorrel
Rumex acetosa

Sometimes called French sorrel or garden sorrel, broad-leaf sorrel is a hardy perennial herb with a sprightly lemon flavor.

Growing

Sorrel tolerates partial shade, ordinary soil, and withstands drought. Plant in an herb or culinary garden, but not for its esthetic qualities. Keep nipping off the flower stems to keep the leaves growing. Tends to bolt like lettuce when the weather turns hot.

Culinary

Old leaves are tough and not as flavorful as the young ones. A favorite for soups, fish, and salads, and makes far more flavorful substitute for lettuce on sandwiches. Cook leaves like spinach as a tangy vegetable. I also pick a few leaves to nibble in the garden as I work to quench my thirst. Sorrel is sometimes used in recipes that call for sour grass.

Varieties

- *Rumex acetosa* 'Profusion', developed by Richters, doesn't go to seed, so leaves are tender and productive all season. An improvement over other varieties, which are tender in spring and early summer only and which must be kept cut down to grow a second crop for early fall.

- *Rumex acetosella,* sheep sorrel, grows wild as a weed. Its small leaves are excellent in salads, soups, and sauces. This perennial can be a nuisance because it spreads from the roots and pops up everywhere. Thought to be useful for fevers, diarrhea, and cancer control.

- *Rumex scutatus,* French sorrel, is a perennial plant that doesn't spread out of control like its unruly cousin, sheep sorrel.

Lemon Thyme
Thymus × citriodorus

This fragrant and delicious species of thyme has small, pointed, dark green leaves and an upright habit resembling a small, low-mounding shrub. The sharp lemon scent combined with that of traditional thyme is enough to make the mouth water. The plant is covered in summer with tiny flowers attractive to bees. The flowers can be white, soft pink, or pale lavender. It grows about 10 inches high and is useful in an herb garden, in front of a border, and in containers. There are other lemon thymes among the creepers *(Thymus serpyllum)* with a low growing habit. Because the thymes are so easy to grow, so lovely in the garden, so delicious, and perennial to boot, they are a must in every herb garden.

Growing

Propagate by division in spring through midsummer and by cuttings from the green top growth. Strip cut ends of leaves, dip in rooting hormone, and stand in damp sand or seed starting mixture until rooted. Keep watered, damp but not sopping wet. Some varieties can also be grown from seed, started indoors in the spring.

Thyme likes full sun and a light, well-drained soil but can tolerate partial shade. It is hardy in zones 5 to 9. The plant is susceptible to root rot if drainage is poor and to fungus diseases. As a native to the Mediterranean areas, it also can stand up well in a dry climate.

Thymus × *citriodorus* 'Aureus'.

Plant the creeping lemon thymes between pavers or flagstones and around steps for the best effect. Both the creeping thymes and the upright thymes are useful in rock gardens and for edging in perennial beds. The creeping thymes are sometimes used in bonsai or topiaries at the base of the pot instead of moss.

Culinary

Harvest a crop for freezing or drying in the early summer; the plant will regrow for a second harvest in the fall. Thyme leaves retain their flavor after drying better than many other herbs. Remember that dried herbs are about twice as potent as the same quantity of fresh herbs, so check your recipe and substitute accordingly.

Lemon thymes are excellent in a small bouquet of herbs in the stew pot, with grilled fish or chicken, or in stuffings, fresh fruit salads, or desserts. Thyme is a primary seasoning in fish chowders, where lemon thyme is even more effective than the species. Use also on salads, in vinegars and dressings, and with egg dishes for added zip. In fact, there are few dishes that won't be enhanced by the flavor of lemon thyme.

Varieties

- *Thymus × citriodorus* 'Aureus', golden lemon thyme, has golden-edged leaves.
- *T. × c.* 'Goldstream' makes a carpet of green flecked with gold.
- *T. × c.* 'Lemon Frost' has shiny green leaves and white flowers that bloom early and again late in the season.
- *T. × c.* 'Lemon Mist' is a low-mounding plant with white flowers.
- *T. × c.* 'Argenteus' is lemon flavored and has lavender flowers and white-edged leaves.
- *T. pulegioides* 'Lemon' is a creeping lemon thyme with a strong scent.
- *T. praecox* subsp. *arcticus* 'Lemon Mother of Thyme' is a lovely ground cover with a dense, creeping growth pattern and pale pink flowers. Grows only about 2 inches high, compared to 10 inches for the upright thymes.
- *T. serpyllum* 'Pygmaeus Lemon', or 'Pygmy Lemon Mother of Thyme', is a minute creeping thyme. Use small creeping thymes like this one to main-

tain proper scale of lawns in model train garden landscapes and for other miniature plantings.

- *T. herba-barona* cv. 'Lemon Carpet Thyme' (Richters) is a very low-growing variety meant to be walked on, releasing its fragrance with every step.

Lemon Tree
Citrus limon

The familiar golden lemon is one of the most popular fruits in the world. The tree is highly decorative, and many are ever-blooming both in the garden and in the sunroom. The clusters of small, white flowers are intensely fragrant, and the shiny, dark green leaves are decorative. The tree has small, sharp spines in the leaf axils. The juice is tart and delicious mixed with other ingredients.

Mature trees grow to 22 feet, but dwarf species are currently more popular for the home gardener. A fully grown tree in the best of circumstances can yield up to three thousand lemons per year.

Citrus limon 'Meyer'.

The tree is thought to have been native to India, then to have spread through Turkey and Italy to the rest of Europe, and also to North Africa and through the Moslem world. Lemons and other citrus were planted in the Spanish settlement of St. Augustine, Florida, in 1565. Spanish explorers also brought the seeds to the New World through Haiti and Mexico, and missionaries extended the range to Southern California when they established their mission gardens.

Growing

Most lemon trees are in constant bloom throughout the year, and depending on the local climate, fruit can be harvested from the garden continuously. In coastal areas where the temperature falls more at night, there is likely to be more bloom and fruit production year-round. In desert areas, lemons tend to ripen in late fall and winter.

Plant 'Meyer', 'Improved Meyer', or Ponderosa' in big pots or tubs on wheels, and grow as tender plants in frost areas, spending summer outdoors and winter in a sunny spot indoors. The very fragrant, white flowers are an olfactory pleasure, and the fruits are delicious. The Meyer lemon is more thin skinned and juicier than the standard supermarket lemon.

Citrus limon 'Meyer' is the right size for a small garden.

If planting a lemon tree directly in the garden, keep grass away from the trunk with mulch. There will be feeder roots very close to the surface of the soil so any digging or cultivating around that area may damage them and stunt the tree. Lemons like a night temperature of 50 to 60 degrees.

Prune to keep growth under control and to encourage a more pleasing shape. 'Meyer' lemons are sometimes used as hedges, and all lemons can be

Citrus limon 'Meyer' in flower.

Citrus limon 'Ponderosa' fruit and flower simultaneously.

espaliered against a wall for decorative effect. Propagate from cuttings of green stems that aren't fully mature in spring or early summer.

Lemon trees can be started indoors from seed. The process is not infallible, but it's exciting. Collect whole seeds from a cut lemon. Try to find one from a dwarf tree like the 'Meyer' or 'Improved Meyer', which are sold in late winter labeled as such in specialty food stores. Wash off the seeds, and let them dry for 48 hours on a paper towel. Plant several in a small pot with loose potting soil. Place in the sun and water when dry to the touch. With luck, at least one will sprout. If more seeds germinate, separate them into other pots and treat as you would a houseplant until time to set outside. Repot as your seedling grows out of its original space. Keep the plants well watered, but make sure they have good drainage. Waiting for the tree to mature enough to produce flowers and fruit takes patience, three to five years at least. Think of it as a nice green houseplant until then.

This 'Ponderosa' lemon makes a statement in a Florida backyard.

Culinary

Lemons have seemingly endless culinary uses. If you grow your own, harvest them when they are fully ripe, or yellow, for the most intense flavor. If the ripe fruit is left on the tree, it develops a thicker skin and becomes less juicy and less acidic, although you may want to leave some for decorative purposes. If purchasing lemons, look for ones that are unblemished, seem to have a thin rind, and are heavy in the hand. That means they are jucier and less pithy than others. Use organic lemons when grating the rind for recipes. Pesticides are difficult to remove with normal rinsing.

Before juicing lemons, remove from the refrigerator and allow to come to room temperature. Then roll on the counter, pressing down with the palm of your hand. You'll increase the juice production by more than a third. When lemons are in season or a bargain at the grocery, buy a dozen or more and juice them. Freeze in ice cube trays, filling about half full, then put in a Ziploc bag for longer storage. Use one by one in recipes as you need them.

If your lemons ripen all at once and you're out of refrigerator space for storage, submerge in bowls of cold water rather than leaving on a shelf, where they will dry out. Here are some handy culinary uses for lemons:

- Squeeze lemon juice over cut apples, bananas, peaches, and pears to prevent browning if they have to sit while you are preparing a recipe.

- Slice fresh lemon into ice water, tomato juice, frozen lemonade, or cola to impart a fresher taste.

- To make your own buttermilk for baking, add fresh milk to 1 tablespoon of lemon juice to make 1 cup. Let stand for a few minutes.

Varieties

- 'Meyer Lemon' is hardy to zone 9 and grows to 3 feet in a container with full sun, or 8 to 10 feet in the garden in zone 9 or 10. It is an heirloom variety, a dwarf tree, and both evergreen and everbearing. It is thought to be a cross between a lemon and an orange or a mandarin and probably originated in China. The flavor is slightly sweet and perfumy, but still acidic. This variety can tolerate occasional frosts to 18 degrees.

- 'Improved Meyer Lemon' is more cold and virus resistant than the 'Meyer'.

- 'Ponderosa', or 'American Wonder' lemon, may grow indoors to 15 feet with care. It has very large fruit, the size of grapefruits, and is hardy to zone 9. It is thought to be a cross between a lemon and a citron. The skin texture is rough and the rind thick; the flesh is seedy, so it is not ideal as a juice lemon. If the tree becomes laden with heavy fruit, you may need to prop up the branches to prevent breakage of the limbs.

Citrus limon 'Pink Lemonade'.

• 'Pink Lemonade' has a green leaf variegated with cream on the edges. The yellow fruit has well-defined lime green stripes. The flesh is pink like a grapefruit, so it's rather exotic looking, but the flavor is pure lemon. Although the flesh is a lovely pink, it's not quite deep enough to make a natural pink lemonade without a color additive. Hardy in zones 9 and 10, this small tree makes a decorative pot plant.

Aloysia triphylla in flower.

Lemon Verbena
Aloysia triphylla (syn. *Lippia citrodora*)

This herb, native to Argentina and Chile, is hardy to zones 8 and 9. It's usually listed as a tender shrub and can grow to 5 to 6 feet in a frost-free environment, and even taller in its native habitat. In colder areas, grow as a tender perennial. It will die when severe frost hits the plant unless brought inside for the winter. There it may drop its leaves, as it is deciduous. It has a strong lemon scent and flavor and is a favorite of mine. The plant has three or four leaves in whorls around a woody stem.

Growing

Grow in loose, well-drained, sandy soil. As a houseplant, keep the roots out of standing water. Plant in full sun, although partial shade in afternoon is best in hotter climates. Add a small dose of lime to acid soils.

It's easy to find small pots for sale at most herb sources, or propagate by taking stem cuttings from the top of the plant in midsummer so they can root before the days grow shorter. The cuttings likely will lose leaves in fall.

Your lemon verbena may go into dormancy and lose all its leaves if there is a rapid temperature change or a dip below freezing, or if the roots have been disturbed by digging to transplant or pot up for winter. Don't toss it on the compost pile prematurely; it likely will recover.

Trimming the tips of the branches during the growing season makes the herb leafier, and it will have a prettier, less leggy form in the garden. Keep the trimmings for culinary or potpourri use. Prune stems even more, as much as halfway down, to harvest even more leaves. You can do this several times during the summer. The harder you prune, the fewer flowers you'll see, but that's no great loss, as the small white and lavender blossoms that cluster along the tips of the stems are insignificant in the garden. This plant is prized for the scent and flavor of the leaves, and the essential oils are stronger before flowering.

Grow in the herb bed or in a mixed flower border where bright greenery is desirable. In Southern California and other parts of the South, you can grow it as a small shrub.

Lemon verbena is also favored as a fragrant herb for an indoor sunporch. It is often trained as a topiary or standard for more formal indoor use. It is very susceptible to whiteflies and spider mites, so wash all surfaces of leaves carefully and spray with insecticidal soap at the first sign of trouble.

Culinary

Lemon verbena has a strong lemon flavor, more intense than that of lemon balm, so if you substitute it for lemon balm, use only half the amount. It is used to flavor desserts, fruit salads, teas, and other sweet drinks. Add a sprig of lemon verbena to a tall, frosty glass of lemonade or iced tea rather than the ubiquitous sprig of mint. This is one herb that is as good dried as it is fresh or frozen.

CHAPTER TWO

Uses of Lemon Herbs

Medicinal Uses

The increasing popularity of herbs as medicines in the late twentieth century into the twenty-first is based on several suppositions: that since all herbs are "natural," they are invariably beneficial; that all conditions can be cured or at least alleviated with the right herb; and that herbal use in centuries and cultures past led to better health than in our own time and place. Herbs probably were undervalued in the last century, as modern medicine became both highly successful and highly profitable, but the pendulum threatens to swing in the other direction, as outlandish claims are being made with no proof and no controls.

Before outlining some possible benefits of lemon herbs, a few warnings are in order:

- Some herbs, even those organically grown, can be inherently dangerous. Monkshood and castor bean, for example, are two herbal poisons.

- Most otherwise beneficial herbs can be poisonous if ingested in too strong a dose. Foxglove (*Digitalis*), which has been used for centuries for heart conditions in its natural and synthetic forms, can also kill. Of course, too much of any food or medicine can make you sick or be fatal.

- People react differently and can have an allergic reaction to relatively innocuous botanicals.

LEFT: A bridal bouquet is transformed into a keepsake potpourri with the addition of some highly scented lemon verbena leaves.

- Babies are in a whole different category from adults. Avoid dosing a baby or a small child with anything not cleared by your physician.

- Much romantic drivel has been written about medicinal uses of herbs based on anecdotal evidence that has no relationship to repeatable, observable fact. If you want to try something that is not known to be harmful, proceed with great caution.

- Growing conditions can change the strength and properties of any herbal; too little sun, not enough or too much rain, age of the plant, or the part of the plant being used can all produce variation in the chemical substance available to the user.

The medicinal uses for many of the lemon herbs are not based on their lemon qualities but on the properties of the underlying species. I have seen no evidence that the lemon thymes, for example, have been tested separately from ordinary thyme.

Lemon Balm

The herbalist John Gerard (1545–1612) claimed that lemon balm "comforts the heart and driveth away melancholy and sadness." At one time, lemon balm was also used for nervous complaints, hysteria, melancholia, and migraines. Some herbalists believe this herb calms the nerves and stimulates the heart.

James A. Duke, in *The Green Pharmacy,* claims it is highly effective against viral infections such as herpes simplex, shingles, mumps, and chronic fatigue syndrome, and to treat fever from colds. For the sores from herpes or shingles, a cream or strong lemon balm tea is applied directly to the sores to promote healing; drinking the tea may be effective as well.

A hot infusion made from the steeped fresh leaves promotes sweating and has a sedative action thought to help insomnia and soothe stomach upsets. (See the *PDR for Herbal Medicines* for dosages.)

Lemon Basil

Chew one or two lemon basil leaves to sweeten bad breath. Other medicinal uses are unproven.

Lemon Catmint

Lemon catmint tea taken regularly may slow the buildup of cataracts according to some sources, though it will not prevent them. It is also a mild tranquilizer. Because of its tranquilizing properties, it is sometimes used shortly before bedtime as an aid to sleep. Catmint is one of the many herbs recommended to relieve amenorrhea, though it should not be used by pregnant women.

Lemongrass

The essential oil of lemongrass is used topically to treat acne. Duke suggests that lemongrass oil contains significant fungicidal properties and is useful to treat athlete's foot, both by drinking a tea and applying the tea bags directly to the sores. As a relative of citronella grass, *Cymbopagon nardus,* lemongrass also has some insect repellent properties. If you grow it, cut and rub on skin while working in the garden or relaxing on the deck. Watch out for sharp leaf edges as you rub, however.

An infusion from the leaves has antiseptic properties, which may also reduce airborne bacteria if misted in the air. It will certainly impart a pleasant fragrance.

Mixtures of herbs often work better than one alone. You might mix lemongrass with other antifungal herbs, such as chamomile, licorice root, and garlic, in a poultice for a fungus skin infection, though your friends might leave you alone along with the fungus.

Sorrel

Sorrel has a diuretic effect and is sometimes used for acute and chronic infections of the nasal passages and respiratory tract. The leaves contain oxalic acid, which gives them their characteristic lemony taste. Avoid eating very large quantities in a salad. I usually mix them with other greens or vegetables to dilute the "dose."

Lemon Thyme

It is thought that thyme strengthens the immune system. It has antiseptic uses, coming from thymol, a chemical that also reduces indigestion and flatulence. Duke claims that thymol prevents blood clots that produce heart

Lemon thyme (*Thymus × citriodorus* 'Aureus') may help strengthen the immune system.

attacks. The lemon thymes are popular for culinary uses because of their taste and for the garden.

Lemon Verbena

Lemon verbena is not thought to be useful in medicine today, but it was once used as a mild sedative, to ease indigestion and nausea, and clear bronchial and nasal congestion.

Beauty Preparations

May or June, when the roses are in full bloom, is the time to select some flowers to dry for beauty products. The lavender soon follows in the garden, and some might be spared for your indoor use. By midsummer, when your herb garden is lush with flowers and scented leaves, it seems easier to cut what you need than when flowers are sparse.

When making herbal infusions for cosmetics, it is best to start with distilled water, thereby eliminating all the additives like chlorine and fluoride that may be placed in your public water supply. If you use organic methods in your garden, you will have no concerns about adding pesticides to your bath water.

Some of the lemon herbs, like lemongrass, enhance skin sensitivity and may cause irritation, so it's always wise to do a patch test before you subject your face or whole body to your preparation. Place one drop of the preparation on the inside of your wrist or forearm, and leave it for 12 hours, checking for redness and irritation.

Another favorite herb, lemon verbena, has photosensitizing properties, making the skin more reactive to the sun's rays. Avoid direct sun exposure for six hours after applying. It's best in the evening bath.

Here are some simple ideas for herbal beauty preparations:

- Make a warm lemon balm infusion for cleansing the face by pouring 2 cups boiling water over 6 tablespoons fresh lemon balm leaves. Cover tightly, steep, and strain. It will keep refrigerated in a closed jar for about a week.

- Lemon juice added to a final rinse water makes hair shine and brings out golden highlights in blond hair. Mothers used to lighten daughters' hair in summer, bleached by sun and a weekly lemon water rinse.

- To prepare a skin cleansing mist, soak 1 cup bruised or chopped lemon mint leaves in 2 cups white vinegar in a covered jar for two weeks, shaking daily. Strain through two layers of cheesecloth or dampened strong paper towel in a sieve. Place in a fine mister to cool and cleanse face.

- Make an herbal bath oil or massage oil starting with 2 cups fresh olive oil, safflower oil, or sweet almond oil as the base or carrier of the scent. Steep a mixture of lemon balm and lavender, totaling 1 cup, in the oil for 48 hours. (Some herbalists like to steep this mixture in the sun, in a sterilized jar, as you would with sun tea, to hasten the release of the herbal oils.) Strain out the herbs and replace them with fresh herbs, steeping for 48 hours again in the same oil. Keep repeating with fresh herbs till you have done this a total of five times. The base oil should now contain a nice concentration of herbal oil. Strain carefully a final time. You can bottle this oil and a use few drops in the bath or for a relaxing massage. Little girls will especially love to make this scented oil for their own baths. For gift giving, collect old bottles and jars with tight lids. Clean impeccably before adding your own herbal oil preparations.

- Make herbal bath bags without the work of making an infusion. Buy 1/2 yard of white netting, like that used for wedding veils, at a fabric store. Cut into 9-inch squares. Use the squares at double thickness for each bag. Pile a mixture of dried herbs in the center. Some herbs of particular pleasure for a relaxing bath are lavender, chamomile flowers, rose petals, calendula flowers, and lemon balm in equal parts. (This delightful recipe can also be used as a potpourri.) Now bring up the corners, and tie with raffia or a small ribbon, leaving the ends long enough to tie to the faucet as the bath is filling; the warm water pouring directly on the bag will help release the aromas. Let the bag steep in the water as you are relaxing. Just before emerging, rub the bag over your body for added fragrance. Bath bags make delightful favors or stocking stuffers, or can be included with other items in a gift basket. Label the bath bag as such and include instructions for submerging in hot bath water. An easier way to make them for your own use is to cut pieces of old pantyhose and tie with string. Not as charming, but they work just as well. Bath bags are meant for a single use, but if you're the type to reuse tea bags, you may do the same with bath bags, allowing to dry out before the second use.

- Use lemon basil in massage oils and herbal baths. It is thought to have a calming effect. Try rubbing the leaves directly on the skin to repel mosquitoes and other annoying insects. It is commonly used in this way in India, and it might work for you.

- Use the dried leaves of lemon verbena to scent bath water or in herbal skin products, like hand creams and massage oils. The lemon scent is invigorating.

Cleaning with Lemon Herbs

Here are some ways you can use fresh lemon herbs around the house to help with your cleaning chores and take advantage of their delightful scent:

- For lemon-scented ironing water, place 1 cup bruised lemon verbena leaves, 1/3 cup sweet lavender, and 3 cups distilled water in a lidded glass jar. Place in a cool, dark place and shake daily for two weeks. Strain through cheesecloth or a coffee filter, and fill a spray bottle to keep near your ironing board. Set mist to fine and spray on cottons before you iron. A faint smell of herbs will follow you wherever you go.

- Throw a few handfuls of crumbled dried lemon verbena or lemon geranium leaves on the carpet before vacuuming. As you tread upon the leaves, they release a powerful perfume, which gets into the vacuum and scents that as well.

- When you are finished squeezing a whole lemon, grind the rind and remains in the garbage disposal to cleanse, disinfect, and deodorize.

- Rub your hands with cut lemons to remove the smell of shrimp, fish, garlic, onions, or gasoline.

- In South Africa, their native habitat, lemon geranium leaves are sometimes rubbed on wood bowls and furniture both to oil and preserve the wood and to impart a wonderful aroma.

- Food stains on kitchen counters can sometimes be removed by bleaching with lemon juice left on the stain for 45 minutes, then rubbing with baking soda.

- Rub copper pots with a mixture of salt and lemon juice for a beautiful, natural shine.

- Fill discolored aluminum post with water and a sliced lemon or two, and boil to restore the shine.

- Squeeze lemon juice on rust stains on white fabrics, and let dry in the sun. Then wash as usual.

Herbal Dry Potpourris

The word *potpourri* means a stew, medley, mixture, or collection. It is commonly used to refer to an aromatic blend of scented botanicals that impart a delightful fragrance in the home. Commercial potpourris, mass produced with chemicals and wood shavings dyed to fool the eye, are as different from a delightful homemade potpourri as a box cake from your fabulous confection baked from scratch. The finest ingredients in potpourris produce fabu-

Lemon verbena leaves add a delicious scent to this rose potpourri.

lous results. And because your garden blooms anew each year, you can replace last year's mixture at almost no cost. As when concocting any stew, the proportions of the ingredients depend on what you have on hand and your personal preferences. A dried potpourri has four basic traits: aroma, color, texture, and longevity.

Aroma

I think a mixture of nothing but lemon geranium leaves will please me to the end of my days, put perhaps a little more complexity is in order. Preference for scents is highly idiosyncratic, and if you share your home with other family members, consider their preferences as well.

Lemon herbs are among the most universally pleasing for potpourris. Their tangy yet sweet smell combines well with spices at fall and winter holiday times and with light florals in spring and summer. For a strong scent, choose lemon verbena, lemon geranium, lemon balm, lemon mint, or lemon monarda. Any of these can be used to provide the major note or as background for another scent, such as a primarily rose potpourri. Lemon geranium emits a glorious aroma when the leaves are rubbed or bruised, but the dried leaves turn brown rather quickly, so use them in potpourris where other elements provide the color. Lemon eucalyptus can be dried for a more delicate scent. Dry the long leaves by hanging. Gently rub the leaves in passing to release the fragrant oils.

Some potpourri makers use purchased essential oils to provide the main aroma in their mix. I prefer to use one or two drops of oil only if I'm seeking a scent I can't grow, like patchouli or sandalwood, or to refresh a scent after about six months. So the potpourri mix must be intense from the start.

In combination with the lemon herbs, for a sweet smell I love rose petals, one of the sweet lavenders like 'Hidcote' or 'Munstead', sweet Annie, heliotrope, lily of the valley, gardenia, or peony. Another great favorite is the small, white flower of the pearly everlasting. For a spicy or pungent mix, try heavily scented carnations and pinks, feverfew, eucalyptus, dried curled bits of citrus rind, tansy and yarrow, sage, silver king artemisia, thyme, or conifer needles such as juniper or spruce. Flowers dried for potpourri do not have to look perfect, but they should retain their basic structure and color and still be recognizable. Broken petals and leaves, which have a stronger scent than whole ones, can form the bottom layer, which will be out of sight even if you plan to lay your flowers out in an intricate pattern on the top layer.

Flowers and herbs should be dried rapidly and kept in the dark until mixed in a potpourri no more than a month later. You are trying to capture the full aroma of the plant. If you store your flowers for too long, until you get around to making the potpourri, they will lose their fragrance.

Color

To provide the visual stimulation of color, try to have some elements in the potpourri be as vivid as possible, even if they contribute no scent to the mixture. Some of the most beautiful displays stay within one color palette or blend into one color range. For my *Lavender* book, I blended an all blue potpourri based on lavender buds, blue hydrangea, and dried bachelor buttons, then added some flowers with complementary colors on the color wheel, bright orange and gold of sunflowers and calendula. The lavender provided all of the fragrance; the other flowers were mixed in for color and texture.

Vary color by season. In the fall, work with autumnal shades of yellow and orange for the top layer. Curls of dried lemon zest provide both color and aroma, and Japanese lantern pods off the stems offer a brilliant orange color in an exotic shape. For Christmas, use green leaves of lemon verbena or lemon-scented geranium with dried red pepperberries and small conifer cones and needles. Make a winter potpourri of snowy white materials, using translucent pods of the money plant (*Lunaria*), pearly everlasting, and white roses, with a mixture of lemon herbs. For spring, use pastels or highlight the colors of sunshine, with air-dried narcissus, so appropriate with the lemon-scented herbs you have grown. For summer, try the hottest mixtures of riotous colors—purples, pinks, reds, and oranges all mixed together.

When using roses, dry varieties with a strong orange cast, like 'Mercedes' or 'Tropicana'. These will dry a strong, clear red that lasts for several years. Softer-colored roses will fade more quickly.

Many of the everlastings, such as strawflower heads, globe amaranth, colored statice, and cockscomb, provide both a strong color and a long-lasting structure to your potpourri. If you don't grow colored statice, purchase a few stems in blue, purple, or hot pink from a florist. Cut off the top few inches. These will dry within days for your mixture. If the heads of cockscomb are too large, you can break them in pieces vertically with great ease.

You can dry your own lemon zest or whole slices of lemon (see page 80) to add aroma and texture, as well as color.

Texture

You can simply blend all the potpourri ingredients together with essential oils and then distribute in bowls or sachet bags, or for a more artistic look, you can blend the most aromatic materials with a fixative and then lay out the potpourri in a low bowl, arranging the most pleasing whole flowers meticulously in a design on top of the smaller leaves and bits.

Add interesting texture to your design by using botanicals that have no scent of their own but are pleasing to see and touch. Among these are small cones of hemlock, larch, or pine; small pods, such as love-in-a-mist, oriental nigella, rose hips, or poppy; long bean-type pods, like locust, Kentucky coffee bean, or catalpa; pussy willow catkins; the bells from a stalk of bells of Ireland; and berries like juniper.

Using whole flowers in the potpourri will add immensely to its visual appeal. Try white or blue hydrangea clusters, buds and leaves of lamb's ears, air-dried roses or peonies, safflower, calendula, pompom dahlias air-dried on a screen—in fact, almost any flower that holds its shape when dried.

Though aroma is usually the starting point with potpourri, one exception is a keepsake potpourri, made of flowers from a special event, like a wedding bouquet, a Valentine posy, or occasionally even funeral flowers. With a keepsake potpourri, the texture and color are all important; indeed, the flowers, usually from a florist, may have little or no aroma. To make one, lay out the dried whole flowers, leaves, petals, and pieces in a beautiful bowl. Add five or six drops of a fine-quality essential oil for scent, if desired.

Longevity

The main problem with potpourris is how to keep them smelling potent. There are a few ways to prolong the life of your precious concoction, but it's best to discard after no more than a year and replace with a fresh formulation. Take this opportunity to blend a different balance of fragrances as you would change an accessory in the room.

Use a fixative to help preserve and prolong the scent of your newly dried herbs. A fixative may add a scent of its own, but its main job is longevity of the mixture. One of the fixatives most commonly called for in recipes is orris root, in either its chopped or powdered form. Other aromatic fixatives recommended by Penny Black in her book *Potpourri* are whole vanilla beans, cinnamon sticks, cloves and nutmeg, and flowers and leaves of chamomile, angelica, sweet cicely, cumin, sweet woodruff and lemon verbena, and coriander seeds. Feel free to substitute one of these for any fixative in any recipe you use, depending on whether you want a sweet, spicy, or pungent note; each has its own unique fragrance. Black recommends mixing essential oils and any heavily aromatic materials or spices with the fixative, rubbing the materials with your fingers, and letting them rest in a sealed jar for about six weeks before adding other petals and flowers for the longest-lasting results.

Other tips:

- Keep out of direct sunlight; light affects aromatic oils.

- When the scent is no longer obvious, stir the mixture and bruise some of the leaves or petals with your fingers to release additional scent.

- Keep the potpourri in a tightly lidded container and open only on special occasions to release the fragrance sporadically and reawaken the senses with a jolt.

- To refresh a scent, use two or three drops of pure essential oil dropped on the botanicals, and stir slightly to mix in. Use a scent that matches and enhances rather than masks what is already there—rose oil on a rose potpourri, lemon verbena oil on one with lemon verbena leaves.

Simmering Potpourris

To impart an immediate fragrance throughout the house, mix up a simmering potpourri. There is a product on the market called a potpourri maker, which is just a small electric pot in which to simmer water and your redolent mixture. A saucepan on your electric stove will do quite as well, but you must be careful not to let all the water evaporate.

Lemon eucalyptus leaves emit their clean and pungent aroma in potpourris and arrangements.

For a simmering potpourri, color, texture, and longevity are not consider-
ations. The potpourri will be used once, often for a special event such as a
party, and then discarded. Aroma is all-important. Start with 3 cups of water
and 2 handfuls of whatever lemon herbs you have in abundance. Lemon
eucalyptus is excellent, as is one of the sweeter lemon scents. Add a few cloves,
some fresh or dried lemon or orange zest, and 1/2 teaspoon cinnamon, or anything else that strikes your fancy. Add dried lemon slices or peel in the fall
months and for Thanksgiving and Christmas. Bring to a boil, then turn to the
lowest simmer, uncovered. It will last for more than an hour, but the aroma
will linger for hours, even after you turn off the stove.

Teas

To make a lemon herb tea, start with 2 teaspoons fresh herbs or 1 teaspoon
dried herbs per cup of water. This produces a mild tea. If you like stronger flavors, increase the proportion of herbs, up to triple the amount. Always use
fresh herbs in season for better flavor. Place in a warmed glass or china pot,
and pour freshly boiled water on top. Let steep covered for 3 to 5 minutes.
Strain to stop the steeping, and pour. Here are some recipes to try:

- Use any of these herbs by itself: lemon verbena, lemon mint, lemon geranium, lemon balm, or lemongrass.

- Mix lemon thyme, orange mint, and lemon verbena.

- Mix lemon mint and lemon balm.

- For a large group use 8 cups boiling water, four Earl Grey tea bags, and 1/2
  cup loosely packed dried lemon verbena leaves. Serve extra boiled water
  on the side for those who like a weaker tea.

- To warm a cold crowd in winter, serve a tea-based hot punch made from 15
  cups boiling water, 1 can frozen lemonade concentrate, 1 can frozen orange
  concentrate, 1 cup dried lemon verbena leaves, and 1/2 teaspoon cinnamon. Keep hot in a soup kettle on the stove or in a large electric urn. Float
  a thin slice of fresh lemon pierced with three cloves in each cup.

- Cool your guests in summer with an iced tea made from 8 cups boiling
  water poured over 6 green tea bags, 1/4 cup lemon geranium leaves, and 1/8

Conjure up any excuse for a tea party, with Mama's Camish Bread and World's Best Lemon Squares.

cup lemon balm leaves. Steep for 5 minutes, and strain. Cool. Pour into glasses over ice, and garnish with sprigs of lemon balm or lemon geranium leaves. Serve sugar on the side.

- Make your favorite iced tea recipe and add 1 tablespoon chopped fresh lemon verbena leaves.

- Make a lemon herb sun tea by putting herbs and water in a large, clean jar. Screw on the lid, and leave in the sun for about 6 hours. While some people swear by this method, I usually decide on the spur of the moment that a glass of herb tea is essential. So I make it double strength, then pour over lots of ice cubes, which dilute and cool the tea for a lovely drink in about 5 minutes.

Lemon Gift Basket

At holiday time, or when you want to give a personal gift from the garden, make a lemon tea basket. Fill the bottom of a basket with crumpled bright yellow tissue. Pile up the items in a rough pyramid, using more crumpled tissue between the items as stuffing. You can also use whole lemons as filler between the items. Wrap the whole thing with cellophane, and tie with yellow ribbon.

Include some of the following lemon herb items described in this book:

- Bags of dried lemon herbs from your garden, labeled, along with a hand-printed recipe card for each.

- Jar of lemon curd.

- Jar of lemon-cranberry chutney.

- Bag of dried lemon slices.

- Bottle of lemon herb vinegar.

- Small container of lemon camish bread or other sweet treat.

- Herbal bath bags, labeled with ingredients and instructions for use.

- Small bottle of massage or bath oil.

You may also wish to purchase one or more complementary items, such as a tea infuser or strainer, a package of cinnamon sticks, a small gift book on teas, or an antique or collectible teaspoon. Use your imagination.

CHAPTER THREE

Lemon Herbs in the Garden

I am not a traditional herb gardener. I plant my herbs here and there, tucked in where there's room, each year moving them closer and closer to my kitchen door. I'm more likely to cook with fresh herbs if my laziness quotient isn't put to too strong a test. I now fully endorse the rule I once foolishly ignored: Herbs must be handy to the kitchen when I need them, not require a 400-yard trek to a distant garden at the end of a tiring day.

Planning the Garden

Your first step in designing a garden is to choose plants that are appropriate to the growing conditions. Determine the horticultural zone where you garden, and select your plants with this zone in mind. Zone maps appear in most seed and garden catalogs and many gardening books, although these will provide only an approximation for your state and town. Ask advice of an expert gardener nearby as to which plants do well in your area.

Individual microclimates exist, depending on wind patterns, solar reflections, and large water features nearby. If your garden will be on a south-facing slope, enclosed or backed by a brick or stone wall, it could be a full zone higher than that of your town in general. Don't be afraid to do a little experimenting. Try planting a favorite that is expected to survive only to the next higher zone. Your luck might hold for several years, until a winter with more

LEFT: Front to back in an herb bed: 'Lemon Gem' marigold, lesbos basil, and cardinal sage.

frigid temperatures. Then, come spring, you'll have an empty space in your garden, giving you one more reason to try something new.

Also determine the hours of sun the plant will receive and whether the soil tends to be moist or dry. Plants that require full sun need a minimum of 5 hours of sunlight a day. Some plants are very vigorous and have a wider tolerance for diverse conditions. Lemon mint, for example, tolerates full sun or partial shade and dry or moist soil.

Prefer Full Sun

- lemon verbena
- lemon catmint
- lemon basil
- lemon thyme
- 'Lemon Gem' marigold
- lemon bergamot or monarda

Prefer Partial Shade

- lemon balm
- lemon mint

Tolerate Partial Shade

- lemon thyme
- lemon catmint
- lemon savory
- 'Lemon Gem' marigold
- lemon bergamot or monarda

Prefer Moist, Well-Drained Soil (but will tolerate drier soil)

- lemon balm
- lemon catmint
- lemon basil
- lemon mint

Grow Well in the Southwest and Tolerate Dry Soil

- lemon balm

- lemon mint

- lemon verbena

- lemon thyme

- lemon monarda

- lemon catmint

- lemon basil

- sorrel

- lemongrass

Have the Best Decorative Effect

FLOWERS

- 'Lemon Gem' marigold

- Lemon monarda, bergamot, or bee balm

- Scented geranium (*Pelargonium*) 'Frensham'

FRUITS

- Lemon tree

- 'Lemon Drop' pepper

VARIEGATED LEAVES

- *Thymus citriodorus* 'Argenteus', white-edged leaves

- *T. c.* 'Aureus', gold-edged leaves

- *Melissa officinalis* 'Variegata', green with gold leaves

- *Pelargonium* × *citronellum* 'Prince Rupert Variegata', cream and white leaves

- *Citrus limon* 'Pink Lemonade', variegated cream leaves and green-striped, yellow lemons with pink flesh

GOLDEN LEAVES

- *Melissa officinalis* 'Aurea', golden yellow leaves
- *M. o.* 'All Gold', bright chartreuse leaves
- *Pelargonium crispum* 'Variegatum Well-Sweep', golden green leaves

Traditional Herb Gardens

My gardens tend to be natural in appearance. I allow plants to stay where they have volunteered. As plants die out, I replace them with others. And yet there is nothing I admire more in another gardener's landscape than a well-ordered and well-tended herb garden. Wonderful, well-worn brick paths, low hedges of edging plants, and artistic features set in the proper scale fill me with delight.

Lemon herbs have their rightful place in any traditional herb garden for their tastes, scents, color forms, habits, sizes, textures, leaves, flowers, and fruit. As with any herb garden, consistent labels help the visitor appreciate what they are seeing.

Many definitions of herbs abound, and I adhere to a very general and inclusive one. An herb is any plant that is useful to man, excepting plants used as foods, lumber, and fuel. Herbs are used for flavorings, scents, medicines, dyes, religious rites, and pest control. The useful part may be the leaf, stem, root, bark, nut, fruit, pod, seed, flower, or an essential oil or gum resin distilled from part of the plant. The plant may be an annual, perennial, vine, shrub, tree, or fungus.

In this most general definition of herb, the lemon tree fits right in. The fruit juice and rind are typically used for flavoring, and the essential oil is used in medicines, cosmetics, and antiseptics.

The Theme

Traditional herb gardens often have a theme and a thoughtful and regular design pattern. During the Middle Ages when herb gardens were planted in monasteries, medicinal plants, culinary plants, and herbs with mixed uses were kept in separate sections. In modern times, planting decisions are sometimes based on appearance alone; plants with compatible heights, textures, or colors are planted together. The theme might be an aroma garden, with plants that are heavily scented for use in perfumery, soaps, potpourris, and cosmet-

A tasty trio: lemon mint, lemon thyme, and perilla.

ics. Other popular themes are herbs mentioned by Shakespeare in his plays and sonnets; herbs mentioned in the Bible; and herbs for the visually handicapped, which include those with sweet perfumes or more pungent scents and those with unusual textures, such as the velvety lamb's ear. Some gardeners favor designs based on particular colors, such as white and gray or blue and lavender garden. A description of a mixed garden of herbs and flowers with the theme "sunny lemon herbs," a visual and olfactory olio of lemon color and scent, appears on page 68.

The Design

The design of an herb garden can be as structured or as informal as you desire. But there is a particular pleasure in wandering through a formally structured herb garden, where the very regularity brings a feeling of peace and tranquility. Squares or rectangles are divided into quadrants, separated by paths of brick, gravel, or another pleasing material. In the center of the gar-

Melissa officinalis.

den is a fountain, sundial, statue, or other focal point. There is symmetry among the quadrants, though they are not necessarily planted in an identical pattern. A hedge or border around each of the quadrants serves to integrate the design, though the hedge around each may consist of a different plant. Repetition of planting augments the feeling of rhythm. For example, each quadrant may have a rosebush in the center and an edging of upright, variegated thyme around the border. Though the other plants within each quadrant are different, they are planted in repetitive patterns.

Other geometric forms can make attractive herb gardens, such as circles around a square, hexagons, or other shapes with a central axis or other crossing paths.

Knot gardens are more intricate both to plan and to tend, because you must pay constant attention to clipping and pruning to keep the design readily apparent to the eye. Plants form little hedges that weave in and out of each other in more or less complex designs. Constant vigilance is necessary to clip off any offending shoots that disrupt your carefully created pattern. Like topiaries, knot gardens are meant for detail-oriented people who like precision and have the time or the gardener to maintain it.

Mixed-Use Gardens

Lemon herbs can be integrated into any garden or border and need not have a special place of their own. Set a few lemongrass plants anywhere you desire a graceful, narrow-leaved grass that will grow 2 to 3 feet tall. It can make a beautiful border around a garden, although it's not winter-hardy in most areas.

Plant lemon balm or lemon catmint as a ground cover in your rose garden to avoid having a bare look around the base of the roses, and these hardy herbs will appreciate some shade from the shrubs.

Try lemon monarda, with its whorls of lavender flowers, in your cutting garden, or plant it in a garden of all pastel flowers for its interesting growth habit and structure.

Lemon Herbs for Butterflies

Many lemon herbs are suitable in a butterfly garden and also attract hummingbirds and bees. Lemon monarda is a prime candidate, as are the lemon thymes and scented geraniums. Lemon balm is particularly attractive to bees.

To attract butterflies and bees, plant lemon monarda in your border.

A lemon variety gives you the added advantage of being able to use it as a fragrance or culinary plant for yourself, not just for wild creatures.

To attract butterflies, plant masses of one of the preferred plants, rather than just one or two plants. Butterflies will be most content with a tall windscreen like a butterfly bush (*Buddleia*) in the area where they gather nectar. Combine plants for a succession of spring, summer, and fall bloom. Butterflies are particularly susceptible to pesticides sprayed on the food source of the caterpillars; use only organic pest controls if you want to welcome and protect many flying visitors to your garden.

Thyme Covers

One of the pleasures of planting creeping thyme is being able to stuff it in crevices in the garden and treat it as if it were a moss, planted between paving stones, in cracks between steps, tucked into little niches. It's not slippery like a moss can be, and the glory is that the thymes bloom with miniature flowers and release their fantastic fragrance when trod upon. Since they're so easy to propagate, you can get started with a few plants grown from seed, purchased, or begged from a friend. Continue making divisions or taking cuttings to keep the plants coming for a never-ending supply.

Creeping lemon thyme can make an unexpected cushion on the seat of an ancient-looking stone or wooden bench. This is often part of the scene in old English gardens. To make one, first cover the seat with chicken wire, leaving 6 inches extra on all four sides to bend up, forming a wire box. Add a layer of gravel, then sandy soil about 6 inches deep. Tuck the ends of the wire toward the interior of the bench so they won't poke the sitter. Set the plants in the soil about 6 to 8 inches apart, starting close to the edges and working inward. When the roots develop and spread, they hold the soil in place. When the leaves cover the soil completely, the bench is ready for sitting, sipping iced tea, and contemplating the mysteries of the garden.

Rock Gardens

Lemon herbs are nicely suited to rockeries, adding their stimulating scent to the garden. If you plan a path through the rockery, you will be able to further admire the typically smaller plants. Lemon thyme, both the creeping and upright species, is perfect for covering soil areas between the rocks. Plant lemon balm, lemon mint, or lemon catmint on steep banks and other areas where it's hard for plants to grow. Lemon santolina, another perennial, has both lovely, fine-cut foliage and flowers, and 'Lemon Gem' marigolds form small, dense mounds of color that seem to be just the right scale for many rock gardens.

Combining Lemon Herbs with Other Garden Plants

When planning a garden, we tend to choose individual plants, favorites because they remind us of happy events in the past or because we're attracted to a color, aroma, or leaf. We often fall for a pretty picture in a catalog but just as often are disappointed because the plant doesn't grow as well as it did for the horticul-turist at the nursery. And sometimes, the camera lies—flowers that appear large and dominant in a close-up photo look like tiny pinpoints of color in a large garden.

If mortar is missing from a stone wall, it's a good excuse to plant small herbs and flowers.

Garden designers suggest planning and purchasing plants in combinations rather than by individual species. Combinations of three varieties often make for the most satisfactory arrangements. Below are some suggestions for winning threesomes for your garden, or you can form your own threesome around a central idea.

- Lemon monarda, pink zinnias, and verbena 'Homestead Purple'. A summer splash of cheerfulness.

- Scented geranium 'Frensham', purple basil, and purple heliotrope 'Marine'. The green-gold geranium leaves show off against the two purples, almost complementary colors.

- Lemongrass, gladiola 'Key lime', and marigold 'Snowball'. The supple lemongrass contrasts with the stiff gladiola spikes.

- Lemon eucalyptus, globe thistle, and bachelor's buttons. Calming blue shades. All three plants dry well for winter arrangements.

Christine Gaffney planted lemon bergamot, zinnia 'Pink Splendor', and verbena 'Homestead Purple' in a spectacular display in her backyard. Butterflies come flocking.

Lemon-scented geranium 'Frensham' and heliotrope 'Marine' make a spectacular combination of color and aroma. (Royal Botanic Gardens, Toronto, Canada)

- Lemon thyme, sunflower 'Teddy Bear', and coreopsis 'Baby Sun'. A sunny combination in a restricted palette.

- 'Lemon Gem' marigold, cosmos 'Bright Lights Mix', and red amaranth 'Illumination'. A bold combination.

- Thyme 'Argenteus', scented geranium 'Prince Rupert Variegata', and garlic chives. A serene gathering of herbs, with the white blooms of the garlic chives enhanced by the white-edged leaves of the thyme and the variegated cream and white leaves of the geraniums.

- Scented geranium 'Mabel Grey', purple coneflower, and round-leaf oregano. Winsome pink and purple tones.

Container Gardening

Containers come in so many materials, sizes, and forms that there is an appropriate one for any situation. They allow you a versatility that you don't have when planting directly in the soil. All of the lemon herbs are suitable for containers. For hanging baskets and where trailing is desirable, use one of the creeping lemon thymes, lemon mint, or lemon catmint. Plant lemon herbs in containers for the following reasons:

- To decorate a patio, balcony, deck, terrace, or paved area. Where there is no natural soil, free-standing containers or window boxes are a must.

- To hang in baskets from trees, lattice, trellis, or decorative hooks on the house or garage.

- To hang from decorative crooks to provide height in an otherwise flat garden.

Lots of lemon herbs, with annuals for color and one blue mist shrub, which winters over.

Mixing herbs in a container is pleasing to the eye and convenient for the chef. Here I've mixed lemongrass, for height and grace; perilla and round-leaf oregano, for color; and parsley, dill, and Cuban oregano, for texture.

- To grow an invasive species you want to prevent from taking over the garden. Included are lemon mint and lemon balm, which doesn't run but drops a lot of seed to self-sow. If you don't want more, keep the pot on the deck.

- To be able to move the plants from time to time to redecorate. You can move containers at will when you are having parties and special events; when they look particularly fine, put them in a show-off spot.

- To protect a species that is not winter hardy by being able to move it indoors before frost. If your scented geraniums stay in their pots all year, moving inside doesn't require repotting. Dwarf lemon trees, lemongrass, and lemon verbena must be protected from frost and are excellent candidates for moving indoors.

Types of Containers

Water conservation is a prime consideration in container gardening. Unless you have the time and inclination to water every day, use plastic or synthetic pots rather than terra cotta, which is porous and allows the soil to dry out rapidly.

Plant lemon mints in containers to keep their roots in check.

Synthetics have another advantage in that they won't crack if they freeze and thus can remain outdoors year-round.

Stay away from those adorable tiny containers that hold almost no soil. Most of the lemon herbs do well in large containers, and the lemon trees need a large tub. Scented geraniums are an exception; they like to be slightly pot-bound and can be buried in the garden directly in the pot that you purchased the plant. When using large containers or tubs, consider placing them on wheel bases if you will need to move them indoors for the winter.

If you like strawberry jars, the lemon thymes seem to do well. Place the whole jar in a saucer and water from both the top and the bottom.

Planting

All containers need excellent drainage. The pot should have one or more holes at the bottom. Without drainage holes, the plants will drown in the first heavy rainstorm. Put in a layer of gravel or small stones, then fill with a light potting soil mixed with organic material such as compost or humus. Compacted or heavy, wet soil can mean death to herbs in pots. Though it may be tempting to put new herbs in last year's pots and soil, each year the soil in containers should be replaced.

You can plant one species to a pot, and cluster the pots in a decorative way. This allows you to adjust watering and sun requirements for each species. Alternatively, you can plant a mixture of species in one large pot. Select at least one for height and one as a trailer, creating a miniature garden design. Vary the foliage color of nonblooming species.

Watering and Fertilizing

To avoid having to water container plants as often, mix hydrating crystals into the potting soil before planting. The crystals are the size of bath salts and soften into gelatin when watered. They absorb up to ten times their volume in water, slowly releasing it as the soil dries out.

Water when the soil is dry to the touch. Water deeply rather than give frequent sprinklings. As each herb has slightly different water requirements, it may be preferable to plant one herb variety per pot.

Many gardeners use hoses with drip attachments inserted in each pot and controlled by an automatic timing system. I think they're useful, but they're unsightly at close quarters.

A horse trough in front of the barn planted with lemon geranium, lemon verbena, and yellow petunias.

Behind Heaven and Earth Spa and Salon, in Pottsville, Pennsylvania, lemon verbena, caladium, pineapple sage, and lavender struggle to find the light.

Although many herbs will grow in poor soils, when they are grown in containers for decorative use, a moderate amount of fertilizer is beneficial to replace what is constantly being consumed. After planting in the container, wait to fertilize till you see new growth starting. This shows that the roots are ready to start taking up nutrients.

Placement of Pots

Stand containers on outdoor steps to give them varying heights. You can achieve a similar effect by raising some containers on inverted pots, bricks, or wooden boxes.

Lemon Herbs as Houseplants

Lemon herbs do more than brighten up the corner of a room—they also provide a delicious scent. Another reason for having lemon herbs in the house is to protect those that are not winter hardy from frost. Why not keep your lemongrass indoors for the winter, where you can cut a few stems to sauté with your stir fry? Why not save that lemon eucalyptus you worked so hard to find?

The first step when bringing pots indoors is to wash all surfaces of the plant leaves with a hose and wipe the pot, including the bottom. Some insects can be discouraged in this way. Spray with insecticidal soap if you start noticing whitefly, spider mites, or aphids. Lemon verbena is particularly prone to pests, so be vigilant when moving indoors. Mist twice a week with the soap to prevent further outbreaks.

Daytime temperatures should be about 65 degrees F. and night temperatures at least 10 degrees cooler, but most people set the thermostat to please their families and not their houseplants, unless they have a greenhouse. If plants are placed on windowsills, take care that the foliage doesn't touch the panes or it may freeze.

By the 1400s owners of French chateaus and estates were adding *orangeries*, glass-walled south-facing rooms with artificial heat, to house their orange and lemon plants brought from China and India. Wealthy Italians were adding *limonarias* in which to store pots of lemon trees over the winter. If you have neither of these, bring plants in from the garden before frost, and about two weeks before the heat will go on in your home, to give the plants time to adjust to their new atmosphere. Plants must adapt to low humidity and low-light conditions. First move them to a shady spot in the garden for five days, where they can get used to reduced lighting conditions. Indoors, place them where they will receive as much bright light as possible. Fluorescent grow lights can be very helpful, but they are not esthetically pleasing.

The plants may drop leaves. Lemon verbenas are notorious for this, and many people toss them, thinking they are dead. Lemon trees may also drop their leaves if the light is not bright enough. Do not fertilize at this point. After the plant begins to recover, in midwinter, use a fertilizer weak in nitrogen (the first number listed), such as 2-10-10, to encourage root and stem growth but not leaf growth. Turn pots each week to balance the light and promote even growth. Scented geraniums must have good air circulation between plants, so don't crowd them, and keep the roots out of standing water, as they are susceptible to root rot.

Indoors, the dryness of the air in most homes is a problem. To increase the humidity, making it more comfortable for humans as well as herbs, set plants, including lemon trees, on trays of wet pebbles, without letting the water actually touch the roots. I put decorative bowls of water on the radiators in each room so that the water can evaporate slowly into the air. The water levels drop an inch or so a day. Plants are near the bowls but not in them.

After moving the pot out in the garden again in the spring, flush the soil thoroughly with a hose to eliminate accumulated salts.

Some gardeners prefer to take cuttings of their lemon herbs rather than bring the entire plant in the house. Take cuttings in late summer from the growing tips of the plant, dip in rooting hormone, and place in a hole made in a soilless mix. Keep the growing medium moist but not wet, watering when dry to the touch. Add a diluted fertilizer only when new leaves push out from the cutting, indicating growth of roots. Cuttings are a way of propagating extra plants or maintaining plants that won't winter over if you don't want to use them as houseplants.

Some of the lemon herbs, such as the dwarf lemon trees, have blossoms that need no help to waft their perfume. Even one blossom can infuse a room with sweetness. Lemon verbena and scented geraniums may not bloom indoors over the winter, but their aromatic oils are primarily in the leaves. These oils are released by gently rubbing a leaf, thereby breaking down the plant cells. The scent stays with you till you wash your hands. Lemon trees indoors are a botanical display in themselves. At any given time, a plant may exhibit flowers, miniature fruits just forming, green fruits of a mature size, and ripening fruits ready to pick and use. For children and nongardeners, the display can be astonishing, and almost the full life cycle is on view at one time. For more detailed instruction on planting and caring for lemon trees, see *Citrus: A Complete Guide to Selecting and Growing More Than 100 Varieties,* by Lance Walheim.

Topiaries and Standards

Lemon verbena and scented geraniums can be trained as standards or topiaries resembling lollipops. Start with a young plant that you buy or grow from a cutting. To grow a standard, prune to a single straight stem, which becomes woody, and pinch off all side shoots. Allow the top growth to become green and lush. When the plant is about 30 inches tall, cut the top growing tip so that the branching will be more energetic on the sides. Turn the plant a quarter turn each week so that it will receive equal amounts of light on all sides and grow straight and even. It may be necessary to stake it with a stick of natural bamboo. After about three years of such treatment, the standard will resemble a small tree. As you nip off the top growth to keep the plant shapely, you may also be cutting off the flower buds, so expect less bloom than ordinarily. If you keep the standard indoors, fertilize during the growing season and stop fertilizing in the winter when natural light is weakest.

Standards are lovely moved outside after danger of frost. They add height and interest to a deck or patio, as the focus of interest is usually at a different level than that of your other containers. Some gardeners place standards among the plants in an herb garden or border for the same reason.

Recommended varieties of scented geraniums for standards include 'Mabel Grey', because it grows to a single straight stem, and 'Prince Rupert'.

A Sunny Lemon Garden

Planting a small garden around a particular theme increases the interest for both the gardener and the viewer. You can be a purist and plant only materials that fulfill the most rigid requirements of the theme, or you can play with

A small lemon-themed garden at Meadow Lark Flower and Herb Farm.

the theme for your own delight. In planting my sunny lemon garden, I allowed myself a great deal of artistic freedom. My goals were to plant some of my favorite lemon-scented herbs and to mix them with other plants that were lemon colored but had a different scent or no scent at all. Since yellow is a favorite color and lemon is a favorite scent, I have the best of both worlds. The cheery yellow of the flowers seems to enhance the aroma of those with the delicious scent.

Many of the lemon-scented herbs have insignificant-looking flowers, and the leaves can be boring if you use only green varieties. This design includes color variation in the leaves of the herbs, both yellow leaved and variegated varieties, as well as variation in the yellows of the flowers.

The sunny flowers include both annuals and perennials, which don't need replanting each year. If you ever want to redesign, you might change the theme entirely by leaving the yellow perennials in place and adding annuals of another color, such as blue.

This garden is planted in full sun. The horticultural zone is 5^1/$_2$. I started with the lemon herbs and realized from experience that despite what the catalogs say, few grow taller than 2^1/$_2$ to 3 feet in my garden, and most are shorter. Therefore, look for fairly short varieties of sunny annuals and perennials. Sunflowers that tower 6 feet or more and cosmos that grow to 5 feet would look inappropriate. As you select your own favorites to supplement or supplant my suggestions, consider height as important as color.

The Lemon Herbs

You can use any of your favorite lemon-scented herbs in this garden. The seven listed here have different heights, leaf textures, and overall habits. Although they all have a basic lemon scent, it's remarkable how variations in the aroma make them seem very different.

- Lemon verbena, one of the tallest lemon herbs, can go in the background of the garden. I love to rub the leaves to release the aroma as I weed the garden.

- Lemon geranium. Not the flower, but the leaf form and color make the scented geranium a must. Cut leaves one by one for desserts and drinks.

- 'Lemon Gem' marigold. The cheery yellow flowers are showy as well as edible.

- Lemon thyme. This tiny, delicate plant, with variegated leaves, can fill in many odd spots. A perennial that will spread but not ramble around the garden.

- Lemongrass. This herb was selected for the arched grace of the leaves, as well as the rustling sound they make in the wind.

Lemon verbena in a Santa Fe garden.

Lemon marigold 'Lulu' in the golden bed of Thuya Gardens, Northeast Harbor, Maine. Companions are daylily 'Stella d'Oro' and lily 'Grand Cru'.

- Lemon balm. A good perennial to help form the backbone of this garden. Cut down in midsummer to force a new flush of fresh growth for the late-summer garden.

- Lemon tree. A dwarf tree in a pot can be placed anywhere in your sunny lemon garden and brought indoors in the winter if need be. Try an 'Improved Meyer' lemon for its decorative, delicious fruit and the heavenly scent of the blossoms all year long.

The Sunny Perennials

- Yarrow (*Achillea*) 'Moonshine'. Clear yellow flowers, less gold than most of the other yarrows. Plants grow 2 feet tall. A very reliable, long-blooming summer plant with flowers that can be dried for everlasting bouquets. Zones 4 to 9.

- Day lily (*Hemerocallis*). 'Stella d'Oro', which blooms late June to September on 1-foot plants, or 'Joan Senior', billed as the finest white but really pale yellow, a fine rebloomer with large flowers on 2-foot stems. Zones 4 to 9.

- Coreopsis 'Moonbeam' (*Coreopsis verticillata*). Heat resistant, blooms all summer, 18 inches high, spreads to 18 inches wide, good for filling in the front of the border. Zones 4 to 9.

- Green lavender cotton (*Santolina viridis*). An herb with pungent foliage and small yellow button flowers appearing in late summer. The flowers air-dry well. Foliage has a slight lemon scent and is thought to be a moth repellent. An informal edging plant. Zones 5 to 9.

- Foxglove (*Digitalis grandiflora*). A pale yellow perennial foxglove. Usually listed as a shade plant, but self-sows all over my garden. Zones 5 to 8.

- Globe centaurea (*Centaurea macrocephala*). Large, showy, thistlelike puffs of bright gold, blooming in June and July. Zones 3 to 7.

- Gloriosa daisy (*Rudbeckia*) 'Irish Eyes'. In the black-eyed Susan family, but has a bright green cone in the center. Grows to 30 inches.

Sunny Annuals or Tender Perennials

- Joseph's coat, or summer poinsettia (*Amaranthus*), 'Aurora'. Green, straplike foliage with a bushy habit, 2 1/2 feet high. Midsummer to frost, the leaves at the top turn a warm yellow.

- Dwarf sunflowers, such as 'Teddy Bear', 'Big Smile', 'Pacino', 'Elf'. Four-inch blooms on 16-inch plants.

- Safflower (*Carthamus tinctorius*), or false saffron. Flower puffs of orange or cream on green pods. Makes a long-lasting cut or dried flower and is of interest in the herb garden as a food coloring.

- Cosmos 'Cosmic Yellow'. Double and semidouble flowers on 12- to 20-inch plants. Good as cut flowers.

- Calendula 'Deja Vu'. A mixture of yellow and gold tones, some with dark centers. Edible herb; use the flower to decorate salads and platters. Has one of my favorite pungent aromas.

- Gazania. Vivid, daisylike flower on a compact plant with silver foliage. Likes hot, dry conditions. Will be perennial where there are no killing frosts.

- Nasturtium 'Peach Melba' or 'Strawberries and Cream', both a lovely lemon shade, with red markings. Compact habit. Grow as an edging plant, in the front of the border, or in a container. 'Moonlight', a vining plant running to 7 feet with $1^{1}/_{4}$-inch pale yellow blooms. Train as a climber if desired. Nasturtiums like full sun and poor, dry soil. Spicy, edible flowers and leaves related to watercress.

- Marigold 'Snowball' or 'French Vanilla'. Hybrid marigolds bred as whites but really a pale yellow. Excellent contrast to bolder yellow-golds in the garden.

- Osteospermum 'Lemon Symphony'. A large-flowered daisy that likes hot, dry conditions.

- Mexican sunflower, *Tithonia* 'Fiesta del Sol'. Heat and drought tolerant, compact, 28-inch plant. The flowers are orange, and now yellow, but butterflies gravitate to them. For a pure yellow but taller variety, select *Tithonia* 'Goldfinch'.

- Petunia 'Prism Sunshine'. Three-inch blooms on 10-inch plants.

- Zinnia 'Envy'. Chartreuse flowers, a true green-yellow, like unripe lemons. Choose another zinnia if you want a truer yellow.

- Snapdragons. Good in cooler climates. Have two flushes of bloom, first in late spring and again starting in early fall, blooming till frost. Cheery yellow with flower spikes.

Shrubs

- Rose, 'Mary Webb'. A David Austin English rose, 5 by 3 feet, with a large, cupped, soft lemon yellow flower and a strong lemon fragrance.

- Butterfly bush (*Buddleia*) 'Honeycomb'. Buttery yellow blossoms on a large shrub for the background of the garden. Attracts butterflies June to November, after a hard pruning in spring. Drought and pest resistant.

Flowering lemon thyme 'Gold Edge' with 'Teddy Bear' sunflowers and coreopsis 'Baby Sun' in a brilliant bed at the Royal Botanic Garden, Toronto.

Container Plants

In addition to planting in the soil of your garden, consider adding a container or two, standing in a place of honor right in the middle of the garden. A lemon tree can serve this function and allows those of us in the North to fulfill our citrus fantasies.

Use a big, frostproof pot for lemon mint to help contain its growth; you'll surely regret it if you plant it directly in your garden soil. By putting it in a pot and keeping it there all year, you can enjoy a well-behaved plant.

Other Herbs

Here are some other yellow-flowering herbs you may want to include as substitutes to those suggested above.

- Lady's mantle (*Alchemilla mollis*). A perennial with chartreuse blooms in shade or partial shade. Both a dye and a medicinal plant, with lovely leaves that catch drops of dew that make the plant sparkle.

- Celandine poppy (*Chelidonium majus*). A dye plant for yellow dyes. Likes shade or partial shade.

- Roman chamomile (*Chamaemelum nobile*). Used as a tea and medicinally.

- Scotch broom (*Cytisus scoparius*). A small shrub with a pealike flower used for making dyes. The needlelike leaves are excellent for drying.

- Saint-John's-wort (*Hypericum perforatum*). Currently popular as a medicinal herb to enhance the body's immune system. A perennial with a small, bright yellow flower.

- Yellow flag (*Iris pseudacorus*). A water-loving herb used as a dye plant and medicinally. Has a lovely brown pod that can be dried and used decoratively.

- Goldenrod (*Solidago canadensis*). A dye plant with beautiful decorative properties. Gaining more favor as a garden plant as evidence shows that this flower does not cause hay fever. Excellent when dried in bud for wreaths and arrangements.

- Tansy (*Tanacetum vulgare*). A hardy perennial with a flower useful for drying in wreaths and arrangements. Also useful medicinally, as an insect repellent, and as a dye plant.

- Mullein (*Verbascum thapsus*). Tall, stately plant with huge, velvety leaves. A biennial useful as a dye plant and medicinally.

Select any of the plants from each of the categories for your lemon garden, keeping in mind horticultural zone, space restrictions, and light requirements. As your perennials and shrubs are developing to their mature size, usually about three years, include more annuals to fill up the space. After the perennials come into their own, you will select only your favorite annuals for the garden.

CHAPTER FOUR

Lemon Herb Crafts

Fresh and dried herbs in home decoration offer an association with taste and flavor, giving us more than visual pleasure. Sometimes the sight is unexpected, and appeals to the eye, as in the lemon Christmas tree. Sometimes it is our sense of smell that is aroused by fresh herbs in fresh arrangements, or with potpourris. Try your own additions of fresh and dried lemon herbs to your other crafts, and I know you'll be pleased.

Drying Lemon Herbs

Cut herbs for drying after morning dew has evaporated, never when they are wet from rain. Bunch half a handful in a rubber band. Open a paper clip so it forms an S hook and hook it around the rubber band. Now hang from a wire or a hook in your drying place.

In order to air-dry successfully, you need three elements: warmth, darkness, and a dry atmosphere. Warmth may come from an attic, basement, closet, furnace room, or the back bedroom that you don't air, even from the rafters of a garage. Try to find the warmest part of your house or apartment, and string a wire to hang up herbs. Aim for 90 degrees if possible.

Darkness is relative. Your drying place needn't be pitch black, but it should at least be dim. Light fades colors as the herbs or flowers dry, and green is one of the hardest colors to keep.

LEFT: Lemongrass in fresh and dried arrangements provides a contrast in form and texture to a collection of sunflowers.

Small bunches of dried herbs and spices decorate my kitchen fireplace and are ready for plucking if necessary.

A dry atmosphere can also be problematic. In the desert Southwest, it comes with the territory, and herbs hung in a warm garage may dry in a few days. In the humid Northeast, where I live, I find that each summer is different. I dry most of my flowers in my large barn, which is not humidity controlled. During a dry spell, I'm in luck for drying, but the herbs and flowers in the garden need rain for growth. During a rainy period, the garden is lush but the drying is slow. Alas, I have resigned myself to my fate.

Some of the lemon herbs are more attractive than others dried for use in wreaths and arrangements. Lemon monarda has lovely lavender flowers; lemon verbena curls and is fragile, but it maintains a strong aroma and excellent color; lemon catmint dries to a gray color with a bluish cast; and lemongrass adds grace to an arrangement mixed in with stiffer stems. Other herbs do not dry well. Lemon basil turns brown, lemon geranium curls and browns, and the single petals of marigolds shrivel.

Dried Lemons

Use dried whole lemons and dried lemon slices in your craftwork. In potpourris, dried lemon peel adds a lovely refreshing scent and has room-deodorizing properties. Select unblemished fruit that feels light in the hand, with a thick rind and a minimum of juice. Although dehydrated fruits last from year to year, they seem to attract bugs or moths, so I prefer to start each holiday season with newly dried fruits rather than those saved from last year. If you want to store dried fruits, put in herbs like wormwood, yarrow, lavender, cloves, or cedar chips. There never seems to be a moth problem when using only the rind, because those creatures go for the pulp.

My homemade version of a dehydrator works as well as the more expensive models.

Drying Lemon Slices

1. Cut slices about 1/2 inch thick, as evenly as possible. Pat dry on both sides with a paper towel.

2. Dry in a food dehydrator if you have one, according to directions. I don't have one and I use my oven as a dehydrator following the process outlined below.

3. Line a cookie sheet with waxed paper, to make cleanup easier. Place the slices on the sheet in a single layer.

4. Turn on the oven to its lowest setting (mine is 140 degrees). If you have an exhaust, turn it on. If not, crack open the door a little. The slices will dry in about 3 hours. It helps to turn them over midway, relining the cookie sheet with clean waxed paper.

5. Toward the end of the time, keep checking and remove any that look like they are browning. It's better to remove slices that are slightly tacky and let them finish air drying in a warm spot, such as on top of the refrigerator or a radiator, than to let them get brown in the oven.

Drying Whole Lemons

1. With a paring knife, make five or six slits in the fruit, starting 1/2 inch from one end and stopping 1/2 inch from the other end. Just pierce the flesh; don't cut all the way through, or you'll have two lemon halves.

2. Dry as for slices, but the whole fruit will take much longer, maybe about 12 to 14 hours, depending on the size and juiciness of the fruit. Don't be tempted to turn up the oven temperature, or you'll have baked rather than dehydrated lemons. If you leave the house or go to bed and don't want to leave the oven on, you can turn off the oven and restart it again later. One side of the fruit may get flat, but turn that side inward when you are designing your craft project.

3. Allow them to finish drying in a warm spot, such as on top of the refrigerator or a radiator.

Drying Lemon Peel

1. Using a zester made for the purpose (the gadget used by bartenders when peeling a twist) or a vegetable peeler for wider, less even slices of rind, peel

Sliced lemons and hot peppers add sunshine to bottled vinegars.

off only the yellow part of the rind with as little as possible of the white, which has a bitter flavor and scent.

2. Either trim the slices evenly and cut into matchsticks, or chop roughly if neatness doesn't count.

Decorative Vinegars

Kitchens are gathering places not just for the hungry, but for those seeking the warmth of the hearth, closeness to the cook, anticipation for what's coming from the oven. The central path to my old stone farmhouse leads directly into the kitchen. Only strangers find the "real" front door, walking on semiburied stepping-stones onto the front porch and then to the front hall. My kitchen is large, with a walk-in fireplace at one end. I sit on an old oak rocker by the window while I drink my afternoon tea, watching the 60-foot catalpa tree transform itself through the seasons.

Since the kitchen is the entryway for family members and company, I like to place fresh flowers or other decorations front and center on the island to greet people as they come in. From the time I can force the first forsythia in January until a hard frost in October, I harvest something new from the garden each week and arrange it casually in a pitcher or teapot. But as winter approaches, I need a replacement for the garden offerings.

WHAT YOU NEED

glass canning jars of different sizes, new or used

new rubber canning seals (hardware store or supermarket)

clear white vinegar

chopsticks, tongs, or other long, thin tool

assortment of hot peppers, small bright fruits, and vegetables

Decorative vinegars fill the need for something bright, long-lasting, and pleasing to the eye. They are attractive and sure to draw compliments. Although they sell in gift and gourmet stores for a hefty price, it's amazing how easily and inexpensively you can make them yourself. I call them decorative because they are not meant to be consumed. The jars are unsterilized, and the focus is more on esthetics than on flavor. If you wish, you can make them edible by sterilizing the glass containers, adding some garlic or other favorite herbs, and focusing on taste. Glass canning jars can often be found at flea markets. Use brightly colored fruits and/or vegetables, such as baby carrots, cherry tomatoes, new red potatoes, lemon, lime, and orange slices. The least expensive brand of vinegar will work perfectly well for this purpose.

1. Pick over the fruits and vegetables, and discard any bruised or discolored pieces. Wash well.

2. Decide on combinations. Use items from your garden or whatever looks appealing at the market. Here I've used hot peppers and lemon slices.

3. The trick is to insert the fruits or vegetables before the vinegar, in layers and tightly packed, with the best sides out. If you fill with vinegar first, the fruits will just float around in the jar. Use chopsticks, tongs, or other tool to help you place the materials where fingers can't reach. Fill to the brim with fruits and/or vegetables.

4. Fill to the top with vinegar. Place a new rubber seal on the jar and close.

5. A grouping of three or more jars in various sizes looks best. Try glass bottles, if you like, with corks. But it takes more patience to place the fruits in a bottle in an organized way.

Lemon Tree Very Pretty

Small Christmas trees often adorn tabletops, windowsills, dining tables, and buffets—sometimes in addition to the grand tree in the living room, and sometimes in place of it. This permanent tree is easily made of natural grapevine or other vine, such as bittersweet, honeysuckle, wisteria, catbriar, or whatever you have available. Any nice vine will work; each will give the tree a different look. The number of strands you need depends on the size of the cage you start with and how full you want the tree to look. The leaves are actually salal, which resemble lemon leaves and are available from a florist.

Fruit and candy provide much of the decoration for the lemon tree. When using glass ornaments as part of the decoration, select small ones in keeping with the scale of the tree.

WHAT YOU NEED

wire tomato cage, cone shaped

long strands of grapevine or other vine

clippers or pruners

florist reel wire or other thin wire

glue gun and glue sticks

fresh salal leaves

Save the tree from year to year to redecorate in the same manner or with a different theme. You can remove the Christmas ornaments and use the tree base for decorations any time of year, hanging Valentine hearts and cards, Easter ornaments, or tiny photos for a reunion or family party.

If life gives you lemons, decorate a tree.

The vine tree is reusable for many occasions.

The wire tomato cages, available at garden centers, come in several sizes. The finished tree will be about 6 inches wider than the cage, and only a few inches taller, so select the size appropriate to your needs.

1. Invert the cage, with the wide part resting on a table. Starting from the bottom, wrap the first piece of vine around the cage, weaving the strands around the uprights to hold it in place. If necessary, use a small piece of wire to tie the end of the vine to the cage.

2. Continue wrapping up the cage with additional pieces of vine. If you want a fuller look, go back to the bottom and wrap on another layer. When you get to the top, cut off the excess.

3. Hang the decorations on the strands of vine with ornament hooks or small pieces of wire bent to an S shape. For the lemon theme, I've used lemon fruit jelly slices, dried lemon slices (see page 80), small ribbon bows, and small glass ornaments. A big bow with long streamers hangs from the top.

4. Glue the fresh salal leaves onto the vine. These will dry in place.

Herb Wreath

Few of the lemon herbs show as lovely a color when dried as the lemon monarda, with its whorls of lavender flowers climbing the square stem. But it takes a steely heart to harvest it for drying, since its color is so attractive in any flower or herb bed and it engenders much excitement among the bees and butterflies enjoying the nectar. I usually compromise by cutting only one or two bunches for drying, leaving the rest to enjoy during its long season of bloom. This wreath design demonstrates my compromise: a mixed bouquet of herbs and flowers, with the lemon monarda added at the end, where it will show the most. The amount of dried herbs and flowers you need depends on what you have and the size of the wreath. Here, in addition to the lemon monarda, I've used anise hyssop, love-in-a-mist, yarrow, roses, statice, larkspur, peonies, marigolds, and globe thistle.

WHAT YOU NEED

16-gauge wire (hardware store)

wire cutters

spool of 22- to 26-gauge florist wire

flower clippers

glue gun and glue sticks

dried herbs and flowers

While there are many ways to construct a wreath, this method, using a single wire frame, is the most economical and versatile, as you can form it round, oval, heart-shaped, square, rectangular, and of almost any size you wish.

To help keep the wreath even, and save you a trip to the herb farm before the end of your project, make up all your flower bundles and lay them out on the worktable before you start wrapping. Count them. Divide them in half. Use half of the bundles to go halfway around the wreath. For wreath beginners, divide in quarters and know that a quarter of the bundles should form a quarter of the wreath. More experienced crafters can just eye the situation and come out even.

1. Cut a piece of the 16-gauge wire with the wire cutters, and twist the ends together to make a wreath the size and shape you want.

2. Tie one end of the spool wire to the wreath form.

3. Cut bundles of flowers and herbs 6 to 8 inches long, about six stems in each bundle.

4. Take a bundle of flowers, lay it on the wreath frame, sticking out at a slight angle, and wrap it twice with the wire. The bundle will now be secured to

Many are called, all are chosen in this fabulous herb and flower wreath, featuring lemon monarda, roses, peonies, anise hyssop, love-in-a-mist, yarrow, marigold, statice, globe thistle, cockscomb, and larkspur.

the frame. Take another bundle of flowers, lay it atop the stems of the first bundle, and wrap that one once or twice.

5. Continue around the wreath in this manner, until you come to the start. Cut the stems of the last bundle slightly shorter than the others, and tuck them underneath the first flowers.

6. Hang the wreath to assess the evenness. Glue additional flowers in places that seem a little sparse. Also glue on those flowers that you wish to highlight—here the lemon monarda, because I have so few.

7. Find a hook, hang up the wreath, and stand back. Look carefully. Give the wreath a quarter turn and look again. Repeat two more times. Usually one aspect looks better than the others. If you are going to add a bow, follow the same procedure. Attach a small wire hanger on the back of the wreath to designate the top.

Lemon Garlands

Make a long-lasting holiday decoration with dried lemon slices, whole lemons or limes, leaves, cones, and other decorative materials. Salal leaves are available from a florist. It's easy enough for children, relaxing for you, and pleasing to the eye. The mechanics are quick and easy. The time-consuming part is gathering the materials.

If young children are doing this project, let them work from one end to the other. If you want a particularly nice job, start from the middle and work outward to either end, matching the materials on each side. To do this, mark the center of your wire and string on one large fruit. Crimp the wire to hold it in place, and string half of the materials to the end. Then remove the needle, and thread the other end of wire and string from the middle out, following the same pattern. You will wind up with a symmetrical garland.

WHAT YOU NEED

dried lemon slices

whole dried lemons or limes

fresh or dried salal leaves or bay leaves

small pinecones

decorative glass beads

dried hot peppers

bows

needle with large eye

plastic fishing line or 22- or 24-gauge copper wire

wire cutters

pencil

String dried lemon slices, leaves, and cones into festive decorations.

Make this garland as long as you like. You are limited only by the amount of materials you have. You can also add cinnamon sticks, nuts, or small dried pomegranates, but you will need to drill a small hole all the way through each one with an electric drill so you can string these materials.

1. Divide your stringing materials in half.

2. Decide on the length of the garland, add 2 feet for wrapping, and cut off an appropriate piece of wire.

3. Thread the needle with the wire. Now it's just a matter of stringing everything on the wire. Use the needle to pierce the whole fruits through slits in the rind, the tough leaves, and the hot peppers.

4. To attach the pinecones, wrap once or twice with the wire tightly around the scales. Because you're wrapping rather than stringing the cones, be sure the other materials are taut before you wrap.

5. When you get to the end, spiral the extra wire tightly around a pencil, then slide the pencil out. You will have a nice, neat decorative spiral to hold the materials in place and hang down from your garland.

6. Hang your garland. Here I used two pushpins. Tie the bows around the pushpins or nails.

Evergreen Door Swag

The aroma of fresh-cut greens at Christmastime welcomes you home in a way that nothing else can. This easy-to-make swag uses a combination of natural materials in warm, sunny yellows. It's faster to construct and uses less materials than a wreath. Evergreens come in a variety of subtle and not-so-subtle shades of green. This is the perfect time to give your shrubs an extra pruning. Trim branches for craft projects and keep your shrubs under control at the same time.

I like to pair blue Colorado spruce with golden arborvitae, golden cedar, or bare stems of yellow-twig dogwood and decorate the swag with whole fresh lemons and kumquats, which will stay bright and perfect looking for several weeks outdoors in cool weather. Even if they freeze, they'll still look good, and they won't turn mushy until they've frozen and thawed a number of times.

WHAT YOU NEED

assortment of fresh evergreens

5 lemons and 7 kumquats

12 strong twigs, 10 to 12 inches long

clippers

3 plastic cable ties, 6 inches long

ribbon bow

Cable ties are handy little gadgets used by electricians and others for tying together loose wires and cables into neat bundles. You can purchase them in small, inexpensive packs at a hardware store. They look and act like white plastic belts with a buckle. They come in many lengths and are easy to cut shorter once tied. Place the materials on the belt, insert the end through the buckle, and pull tightly. If you've done this correctly, it will not loosen up again. If it does loosen, turn the belt over and buckle it backwards. You'll hear a little ratchet sound as the belt tightens. It will never come loose if tightly pulled. If you want to redesign the bundle, you must cut off the old one and start again.

Greens dry out as they hang and the stems shrink. If you pull the ties really tightly, there is no danger that your swag will fall apart as it gradually shrinks.

And the twigs inserted in the fruit gradually swell with the moisture in the fruit and help keep the citrus firmly attached.

1. Cut one end of each twig to a point. Insert a twig into the end of each lemon and kumquat.

2. As this is a double, or two-tipped, swag, make two separate bundles of evergreen materials, one about 24 inches long and one about 10 inches long. Form each bundle in a roughly fan shape, with the longest branch in the center and shorter branches on the sides. Cut stems as necessary to do this.

3. Cut the "stems" of the lemons and kumquats. Add three lemons and four kumquats to the long bundle, and two lemons and three kumquats to the shorter bundle.

4. As you finish each bundle, secure with a cable tie.

5. Then lay the two bundles end-to-end with their stems overlapping and secure the whole swag with another cable tie. Cut off the excess from the end of the cable tie.

6. Tie the bow in the center, hiding the bottom of the branches and the cable ties.

7. Of course you can make the project even easier by making a single rather than a double swag. Make one bundle, secure with one cable tie. Add a bow, letting some of the stem ends show over the top of the bow.

Lemon Rind Cups

Make about six of these rind cups, and use them at your next tea party to hold goodies like candied citrus peel, cinnamon sticks, or other spices that you use in small amounts. You can also use lemon, orange, or grapefruit rind cups to hold birdseed on a bird feeder wreath. Before the rind dries and becomes too hard, poke a piece of wire through two sides of the top of the cup to form a handle. These baskets are colorful hanging from a wreath that also contains sunflower heads with seeds, small mesh bags of suet, and pinecones smeared with peanut butter.

1. Cut a thick slice off one end of each lemon. You want these to stand up properly on a table, so cut the slice off the most pointed end. Then cut a

very thin slice off the opposite end, just enough to shave off the point but not cut through to the flesh.

2. Scoop out all the flesh into a small bowl, using a spoon or grapefruit knife to scrape out the last bits. Use this juice and flesh for cooking.

3. The cup must now dry in some warm spot in your house. Stuff it loosely with napkins, paper towels, or newspaper, so it will hold its shape as it dries. Remove the paper after about a week so the inside of the cup can dry as well as the outside.

Lemons as a Flower Support

In a crystal punch bowl or pitcher, use fresh, whole, sound lemons to add a decorative note and help support the stems of an arrangement. You also can mix lemons with other citrus, or use red or green apples or cranberries in the same way for a festive look for the holiday season. The fruit will usually last about three weeks, depending on the room temperature, far longer than the fresh flowers in the arrangement.

1. Use only unblemished fruit, as it will last longer. Wash the fruit in soapy water and rinse well.

2. Load into a crystal vase or punch bowl, filling almost to the top. Add water to just cover the lemons.

3. Arrange the flowers and greens as desired, tucking the stems between the fruit to hold it in place.

Fresh, Whole Lemons in an Arrangement

When you need to add color or punch to an arrangement, especially in winter, when the garden is bare, try adding three to five fresh, whole lemons.

1. Find sturdy twigs about 12 to 18 inches long, and shave one end of each to a point.

2. Pierce each lemon about halfway through with a twig.

3. Cut the "stems" to the length needed to add to your other flowers and greens. These lemon stems are top-heavy, so be sure your mechanics in the vase are sturdy, or keep the lemon stems one of the shorter elements in the arrangement.

Whole lemons support the stems of marigolds, zinnias, perennial sunflowers, calendula, and wild goldenrod, keeping them where I want them.

A refreshing whiff of lemon verbena cools down the hot pink of late zinnias and dahlias in this casual arrangement.

Fresh Herbs in Arrangements

We rarely think of using fresh-cut herbs in arrangements, but they can add a delightful note. You can use them instead of the usual green foliage, but their main purpose is their strong fragrance. Here I've combined lemon verbena with summer flowers from my garden in an informal, garden-style bouquet. Lemon verbena is one of my favorite aromas, and I rub the leaves as I walk by to release the scent into the room.

Any one of the lemon geraniums will serve the same purpose with another absolutely delicious scent. Cut stems from those planted in your garden, and the plant will bring forth new growth while you enjoy the aroma indoors.

Pay attention to the leaf color as you design your arrangements. Yellow-tinted leaves combine well with golden flowers or with purples, green leaves with pinks and reds.

Cutting lemon balm for the vase will not only add a happy aroma in the house, but also helps cut down on its weedy look in the garden, where the plant will send out a new flush of growth once cut.

The leaf of the lemon thyme is tiny and the stems are short. Thyme works well in a bud vase with one or two blossoms, an arrangement in a teacup or wine goblet, or a real miniature as small as a thimble. Lemon thyme releases a powerful aroma when bruised.

The aroma of lemongrass is mainly in the base part of the stem, so rubbing the leaf does little good to release aroma in this case. Lemongrass is a perfect choice as a flowing element to soften up the rather stiff and bold look of sunflowers.

The lemon monarda can hold its own in any mixture of cut flowers. It can be hard to decide whether to cut it for summer arrangements, cut it to dry for winter designs, or leave it in the garden to enjoy its color and to attract hummingbirds and butterflies, and then drop seed for next year. Plant an abundance, and you will have enough for all purposes.

CHAPTER FIVE

Cooking with Lemons and Lemon Herbs

L emon herbs are at the top of my list of flavoring ingredients, with garlic and chocolate coming second and third. Unlike most other flavorings, lemon is versatile enough to be used in any course of a meal—appetizer, soup, main course, or dessert—as well as beverages.

Lemon Zest

Lemon rind has two parts: the zest (the yellow outer shell), and the pith (the white inner layers). The pith is bitter and will change the flavor of the finished product. It should be avoided in recipes that call for grated, minced, or chopped lemon rind. When grating, keep rotating the lemon so you collect only the zest, leaving the pith on the fruit. For chopping and mincing, use a sharp paring knife, carrot peeler, or zester to cut off the thin outer layer.

Juice from Whole, Fresh Lemons

An average lemon yields about 2 tablespoons of juice. The juice is a good source of vitamin C and has antioxidant properties, which is why it is often used to prevent cut peaches, bananas, and other fruits from discoloring.

LEFT: The chocolate version of the lemon squares is a guaranteed hit.

Flavorful fruits, organically grown, ready for the kitchen.

Lemon juice, like lime juice, is used as a way of "cooking" raw fish and other seafood in dishes from South America and the Pacific Islands. You can watch scallops marinating in lemon or lime juice for seviche turn from translucent to dull white, as though they have been cooked.

One gallon of lemon juice produces 1/3 to 1/2 pound of citric acid, a sour white compound also found in other citrus and acidic fruits, such as cranberries or currents. Citric acid is used in making flavoring extracts, dyes, and food additives.

If you use small dashes of fresh lemon juice often, cut a small slice off one end of a lemon. Prick the exposed flesh of the whole fruit with a fork. Squeeze drops as needed. Put the lemon back in the refrigerator after use, replacing the end slice, which serves as a little lid. Alternatively, you can buy a little gadget in specialty food stores that screws into the flesh of the lemon and has an attached lid to close the opening. Remove from the refrigerator for each use, open the lid, and squeeze out a few drops as needed. In the sixties and seventies, mesh bags of lemon were sometimes packed with these gadgets made of green plastic as a sales promotion. Now they're manufactured in stainless steel for the same purpose.

Preserving Herbs for Cooking

Freezing

Wash herbs and let dry on the counter. When completely dry, stuff in Ziploc freezer bags and press the air out before sealing. Label the bags. You may think you'll remember what they are, but it's hard months later, when you see only frozen green leaves.

When cooking with frozen herbs, remove the leaves from the stems before adding to most recipes. If you plan to strain the recipe, like a soup or sauce, or to remove the herbs before serving, as in a bouquet garni, you can use the whole stem with leaves intact.

Air Drying

Pick herbs for drying in the morning, if possible, after any dew has evaporated. The volatile oils that provide the flavor are most concentrated before flowers form.

Lemon thyme (*Thymus* × *citriodorus* 'Aureus') is one of the most versatile of all the herbs.

Shake off dust and any insects. Pick off damaged or yellowing leaves. Bring herbs indoors, rinse, and shake. If you grow your herbs organically, this step can be very brief.

Allow the water to evaporate. Then either bunch by the handful in rubber bands and hang in a warm, dark, dry spot, or if you plan to save only the leaves and discard the stems, spread them on a clean piece of mesh screening reserved for this purpose, and set the screen in a warm, dark, dry spot.

Too much heat leads to a loss of flavor. Don't let the heat get over 95 degrees. If you have a gas oven, the pilot light alone may be enough to do the trick.

A food dehydrator can be useful for drying herbs, following the manufacturer's instructions for your appliance. Again, too much heat will diminish the flavor.

The microwave will dry herbs but often ruins the flavor completely by overbaking. I never use the microwave for drying either herbs or flowers, as other methods are much more reliable and produce a consistently better product.

When the herbs are totally dry, store in small, airtight jars, well labeled with variety and date. Always store all herbs in a dark, cool, dry spot, not on spice shelves where they look so attractive. In the light, they lose flavor quickly.

Store different flavored teas individually, or the flavors and scents will merge, and strong scents like mint are likely to overpower more delicate ones. Old English tea caddies, which had three compartments, were not the best way for storing prized teas, as the flavors could easily mingle.

Tips for Cooking with Lemon Herbs

- For flavor equivalents, one part dried herbs equals two parts fresh herbs.

- Frozen herbs always taste better than the same herb dried.

- We often keep dried herbs in our cupboards much too long. The flavor is greatly diminished after a year.

- If you want to reduce or omit salt from a recipe, add lemon juice, garlic, or lemon herbs as replacement.

Recipes

These recipes rely on flavors from the herb garden and lemons from the supermarket except on the occasions I have a Meyer lemon ready for plucking from my tree. The ingredients list is short as is the preparation time, though cooking of a pot roast cannot be rushed. I generally have an eye for low-fat ingredients, although desserts are an exception.

Sorrel Soup

When large groups come to my farm in the spring for lunch and a tour, I always serve this easy, tasty soup, made with fresh sorrel from the garden. It's so quick that I can make it as part of a cooking demonstration and serve it within 30 minutes.

INGREDIENTS

4 cups canned chicken broth

2 cups fresh sorrel leaves

28-ounce can plum tomatoes

3 sprigs fresh thyme

3 garlic cloves, peeled and crushed

1 cup chopped lovage or celery

The classic French sorrel soup is a thick soup that looks much like crème of spinach. I prefer this much lighter version, for which I use low-salt chicken broth. The proportions in this soup are not critical; add more or less of any ingredient to taste. Other vegetables may be added as desired.

Wash and roughly cut sorrel leaves. Roughly dice tomatoes. Combine all ingredients in a soup pot. Bring to a boil, and simmer for 15 minutes. Season to taste with salt and pepper. Remove sprigs of thyme and serve.

Makes 8 cups of soup.

Yia Yia Marista's Avgolemono Soup

Eileen Tognini sent me her mother's recipe for this Greek lemon soup. Her mother and friends still do serious Greek cooking, using time-honored dishes with traditional techniques. I'm trying to wangle an invitation.

Boil chicken broth in a large pot. Pour rice into boiling broth, lower heat, and cook till tender. In a small bowl, mix cornstarch with milk until smooth. Pour into simmering soup, mixing constantly until broth thickens and cloudiness clears. In a medium bowl, beat the yolk with the cold water until thick and foamy. Add the lemon juice. Pour two ladles full of soup into the egg mixture while stirring continuously, then pour back into the soup pot and stir. Serve with a little chopped parsley if desired.

Adding egg to a hot liquid must be done very slowly to avoid coagulating the egg. The traditional method as described here is to add small amounts of hot liquid to the egg, and then pour the whole back into the pot, where the warm egg acts as a thickener. In this dish, the consistency is as important as the flavor.

Some cooks use the whole egg rather than just the yolks. In this case, you must pour the hot soup even more slowly into the egg mixture while stirring continuously to prevent coagulating. I've done this myself many times and can testify that the flavor is still excellent.

INGREDIENTS

6 cups fresh chicken broth, or 14-ounce cans and 3 cups water

$^1/_2$ cup long-grain rice

3 teaspoons cornstarch

$^1/_4$ cup low-fat or skim milk

2 egg yolks

4 tablespoons cold water

juice of one small lemon (more if desired)

Sorrel pesto appetizer packs a punch of flavor with a modest calorie count.

Use extra pine nuts and basil to garnish the plate.

Sorrel Pesto Appetizer

This low-fat appetizer is much like a crustless quiche. Cut in larger portions, it makes a tasty main course for luncheon.

Preheat oven to 325 degrees. Wash and chop sorrel leaves. Cook in boiling salted water for about a minute, until tender. Drain well in a strainer, squeeze out additional liquid, and pat dry with a paper towel. Let cool. Drain cottage cheese in sieve and press out excess liquid. Put all ingredients except pine nuts in food processor, and blend until smooth. Then mix in nuts. Adjust seasonings. Bake in a buttered, 9-inch round pan for about an hour, until lightly brown on top. Let cool. Garnish with small fresh sorrel or basil leaves and small cherry tomatoes, both red and yellow, if you have them. Cut in wedges. Serves 12 as an appetizer, 8 for lunch.

INGREDIENTS

2^1/$_2$ cups nonfat cottage cheese

4 cups fresh sorrel leaves

8 ounces low-fat cream cheese, cut in pieces

^{1}/$_3$ cup grated Parmesan

2 large eggs

2 garlic cloves, minced

4 teaspoons chopped fresh basil

^{1}/$_2$ cup pine nuts

salt and pepper to taste

Herbed Yogurt Cheese

This tangy cheese takes less than 5 minutes in preparation time. Serve with crackers or crisp bread, or with a fresh vegetable platter as a dip. Lemon thyme, lemon basil, and coriander make a winning combination, or use just one or two of these. Vary the combinations as your herbs are available.

Line a sieve with a double layer of rinsed cheesecloth, an unbleached paper coffee filter, or a dampened strong, paper towel. Place the sieve over a bowl. Pour yogurt into the sieve and let drain in the refrigerator for 24 hours, after which it will have lost about half its volume in liquid. Then mix in the chopped fresh herbs and enjoy. Makes about 1 cup. Keeps in the refrigerator for about a week.

INGREDIENTS

16 ounces plain yogurt, with no added gum or gelatin

2 tablespoons fresh herbs, washed, dried, and finely chopped

Lemon Herb Vinegar

Herbal vinegars are so easy and inexpensive to make at home that I can't help but wonder who buys those expensive bottles in specialty stores. Try lemon basil with lemon thyme, or lemon geranium.

Pour into a sterilized jar. Cap the jar, put it in a dark place, and leave it for two weeks, shaking daily (or when you remember). Then line a funnel with an unbleached paper coffee filter or a dampened strong paper towel, and strain into a sterilized bottle. The flavor is already there, but you may want to add several sprigs of fresh herbs and/or some garlic cloves, peppercorns in varying colors, or a tiny hot pepper for a more decorative effect. If giving as a gift, tie a label with raffia to the neck of the bottle. Multiply quantities as desired.

INGREDIENTS

1 cup fresh herb leaves, chopped or bruised

2 cups white or wine vinegar

INGREDIENTS

1 shallot or small onion, minced

2 tablespoons butter

1 pound fresh fish fillets

$^1/_2$ cup dry white wine

2 cups sorrel leaves, stems removed

Poached Fish with Sorrel

This is an easy method for poaching fish, without special equipment. It's one of the fastest-cooking dishes I know. This recipe is excellent with salmon, flounder, or tilapia.

Sauté shallot or onion in butter in a 12-inch saucepan until translucent. Place fish in the pan, and pour wine over it. Wash, drain, and dry sorrel with a paper towel, then chop roughly. Place over fish. Put lid on pan and bring wine to a boil. Reduce heat immediately and simmer, covered. Cooking time depends on the thickness of the fillets and your preference for doneness. I usually undercook fish, and 5 minutes is often enough; 10 minutes should be a maximum. The sorrel should be limp but not mushy. The wine sauce will be thin. If desired, thicken with 1 tablespoon cornstarch dissolved in 1 tablespoon wine. Serve over plain white or brown rice to absorb sauce.

You can use sorrel much the same as spinach. Sorrel is more lemony, but the texture and cooking time of the leaves are very similar. Some people cannot tolerate large quantities of sorrel, however.

INGREDIENTS

2 cups diced, cooked chicken or turkey

1 cup chopped celery or lovage

1 cup seedless red grapes

$^1/_2$ cup walnuts, pecans, or sliced almonds

8 ounces plain low-fat yogurt

$1^1/_2$ tablespoons honey

1 teaspoon fresh lemon thyme

1 teaspoon chopped fresh lemon basil

Herbed Chicken or Turkey Salad

Yogurt makes an excellent substitute for mayonnaise in this delicious, low-fat main course salad.

Mix all ingredients together and serve immediately. You can add any other fruits you'd like, such as bananas, apples, pears, cantaloupe, honeydew, peaches, or plums. It's best to make just the amount you will consume for your meal, as yogurt tends to get watery by the next day, although the salad is still tasty as a leftover. Recipe makes 4 or 5 servings.

Sweet-and-Sour Pot Roast

Various cooking traditions combine meat and sweet fruits. In this dish, lemon provides tartness to balance the sweetness.

In a Dutch oven or enamel pot, brown the meat on all sides in the fat. Remove and set aside. Sauté the onions in the pot until lightly browned. Put the meat back in the pot along with the rest of the ingredients. Bring to a boil. Cover and simmer on top of the stove for 3 hours, or roast at 300 degrees for 3 hours, until the meat is fork tender. Adjust the seasonings about halfway through the cooking. Allow the meat to sit for 30 minutes before slicing. Serve on a platter garnished with twisted lemon slices, so that diners can anticipate the flavor. As with any pot roast, the flavor improves the next day, and leftovers make excellent lunchtime sandwiches.

INGREDIENTS

3 pounds bottom round or chuck roast

a little butter, margarine, or other fat for browning the roast

2 large onions, sliced thin

4 garlic cloves, peeled

1 cup sliced celery

14.5-ounce can diced tomatoes

1/2 cup dry red wine

1/8 teaspoon nutmeg

1/4 teaspoon cinnamon

2 tablespoons brown sugar

2 tablespoons lemon juice

1 cup dried, pitted prunes or mixture prunes and dried apricots

salt and pepper to taste

Slice into lemongrass stalk to release the magical flavor.

Compare the fruits: left to right, the striped 'Pink Lemonade', two 'Meyer' lemons, the large and rough 'Ponderosa', and the familiar supermarket lemon, 'Lisbon', used in lemon oils.

INGREDIENTS

1 pound beef flank steak

2 tablespoons canola or vegetable oil

3 garlic cloves, minced

3-inch piece of ginger, chopped fine

1 yellow or red bell pepper, sliced thin

1 cucumber

5 stalks of lemongrass, white part only, chopped

1/4 cup chopped fresh lemon basil

1 tablespoon chopped fresh cilantro

1/4 cup scallion, cut in thin strips

1/4 cup lime juice

1 tablespoon soy sauce

1/2 cup dry-roasted peanuts or cashews

Beef Salad with Lemongrass

Some main flavors of Thai cooking are here, as interpreted by an American with limited availability of ingredients.

Seed the bell pepper and thinly slice. Peel the cucumber, cut in half lengthwise, scoop out the seeds, and slice. Grill or broil the beef. Allow to sit for 30 minutes, then slice thinly on the diagonal. In a wok or 12-inch saucepan, stir-fry the ginger, bell pepper, cucumber, lemongrass, and lemon basil in the oil until crisp-tender. Remove from heat. Add the lime juice, cilantro, scallion, soy sauce, and nuts. Place beef on lettuce leaves, and spoon nut mixture on top. Equally good served warm or at room temperature. Makes 4 servings. For variety, substitute grilled chicken or shrimp.

Lemon Cranberry Chutney

My friend Gladys Santee gave me this recipe, accompanied by a jar of the chutney to enjoy. Now that's the way to give out recipes! This is a great make-ahead recipe for a special dinner or for giving as a gift. It's a long keeper in the refrigerator or in sterilized canning jars. Use as a relish to pep up the flavor of any plain roasted meat or fowl, or any grain dish.

   Grate the zest of the lemon and set aside. Peel the white from the whole lemon and discard. Cut the lemon in half, remove seeds, and dice. Combine all ingredients except walnuts in a stainless steel saucepan. Bring to a boil. Stir to dissolve sugar. Simmer until cranberries pop and chutney is thickened. Cool and add walnuts. Makes 12 servings.

INGREDIENTS

1 medium lemon

12 ounces fresh cranberries

2 tablespoons grated fresh ginger

$1/2$ cup finely chopped onion

1 small jalapeño pepper, seeded and minced

1 garlic clove, minced

$1/2$ teaspoon cinnamon

2 cups sugar

$1/2$ teaspoon dry mustard

$1/2$ teaspoon salt (optional)

$1/2$ cup chopped walnuts

Lemongrass Sauce

These quantities make only $1/3$ cup, but the sauce packs a big wallop. You can double the recipe to use the following week, keeping refrigerated. It tastes like an exotic teriyaki sauce and can be used as a marinade or brushed on foods before grilling.

   Cut the green tops and any roots off the lemongrass, trimming as you would a leek. Chop finely. Mix all ingredients together. Brush on chicken or fish 30 minutes before roasting or grilling. You can make the recipe even easier by reducing it to the big four: lemongrass, lime juice, brown sugar, and garlic.

INGREDIENTS

6 stalks fresh lemongrass

3 garlic cloves, minced

3 shallots or 2 chives, minced

1 jalapeño pepper, seeded and minced

3 tablespoons fresh lime juice

2 teaspoons brown sugar

$1/2$ teaspoon Tabasco sauce

INGREDIENTS

2 ounces butter, softened to room temperature

1 cup sugar

3 large eggs

2^1/2 cups all-purpose flour

1 tablespoon baking powder

^{1}/2 teaspoon salt (optional)

zest of two lemons

juice of two lemons

Forming the batter with floured hands into three loaves is a sticky job.

Mama's Camish Bread

In the Italian tradition, it's biscotti. In the Jewish tradition, it's camish bread or mandelbrot. By any name, it's a slightly sweet, hard, twice-baked treat to dip in your tea or coffee, or simply crunch. It keeps for ages in a cookie tin and is excellent for mailing to your children away at camp or college. Mandlebrot refers to the sliced or chopped almonds traditionally used in the batter, but you can use almost any other flavoring. In this recipe, lemon dominates.

Cream butter and sugar, add eggs, then add other ingredients in order and mix. Lightly butter a cookie sheet. With your hands, form the mixture into three loaves, about 2 inches in diameter, and place them on the cookie sheet. Bake for 30 minutes at 375 degrees. The loaves will flatten and spread as they bake. Cool on a rack and slice ^{1}/2 to ^{3}/4 inch thick. Reset oven to 300 degrees. Place the slices cut side down on the same cookie sheet. Toast in the slow oven until lightly brown, about 30 minutes. Halfway through the toasting, turn the slices over and let brown on the other side. Cool. Store in a cookie tin to keep crisp.

Camish bread cries out for your special touch. Add ^{1}/4 cup chopped lemon balm leaves for additional lemon flavor with a slightly different note. Or add ^{1}/2 cup golden raisins, sliced almonds, coconut, or mini chocolate bits. Change the flavor as well with small quantities of your favorite spices, such as cinnamon, cardamom, or anise. Treat the whole batch the same way or divide the dough into three bowls

Cool the loaves before slicing and toasting in the oven.

Lemon camish bread with almonds is perfect for dunking in a cup of hot tea.

and make different additions to each loaf before you form it, adjusting the quantities of flavorings proportionately.

Candied Lemon Rind

We can enjoy all parts of the lemon, and the rind is no exception. The yellow outer rind carries the desirable flavor, but the white inner part is bitter. A few strips of candied lemon rind make a refreshing sweet treat after a big dinner.

Fill a 3- to 4-quart saucepan with water, and bring to a boil. Cut a thin slice of rind off each end of the lemons. Then cut each lemon vertically through the stem end, making four cuts, piercing the rind. Peel off the skin. Reserve the pulp for later use. Scrape off some of the white pith from the inside of each wedge of rind and discard. Cut the trimmed rind into neat strips about $1/4$ inch wide. Submerge strips into boiling water, keeping underwater with a spoon for 2 minutes. Drain rind. Change the water in the pot, bring to a boil, and repeat the previous step. Drain rind and boil in fresh water one more time. Drain. Now boil 4 cups of the sugar with 4 cups water over medium heat until sugar has dissolved. Add rind to the pot and keep submerged with a spoon. Continue boiling until candy thermometer reaches 238 degrees and the rinds become translucent. Remove with a slotted spoon, and place strips on a cake rack with a sheet of waxed paper beneath to catch the drips. Let dry until slightly sticky, about 12 hours. Toss candied rind in the remaining cup of sugar to coat, and finish drying on the rack until totally dry. Store in a cookie tin in a cool, dry place, but do not refrigerate.

Candy orange, lime, or grapefruit rinds in the same way. 'Meyer' lemons have particularly flavorful rinds. For gift baskets, package mixed candied rinds together for a colorful blend in a cellophane bag. Such bags are available among the candy-making supplies at any craft store.

INGREDIENTS

6 large, unblemished lemons

5 cups sugar

water

Citrus Ring Cake

A version of this recipe came with my Teflon-lined bundt pan many years ago. It is such a favorite among my dinner guests for its moist, sweet-tart flavor that I made it as a seventieth birthday present for a dear friend who doesn't bake. The cake is rich, sweet, dense, and delicious. It's very easy to slice thinly after it cools and can be cut in 12 or more servings.

Preheat oven to 325 degrees. Whip egg whites until stiff but not dry. Set aside. With the same beaters, in another bowl, cream butter and cup of sugar. Add egg yolks, sour cream, and grated rinds, and beat until light and fluffy. Sift flour, baking powder, and baking soda together and stir into egg yolk mixture. Fold in beaten egg whites. Butter and flour a nonstick bundt pan or ring pan. Bake for 1 hour.

While the cake is baking, make a hot citrus syrup. Mix $1/2$ cup sugar with orange and lemon juice and Grand Marnier or Cointreau. Boil until sugar is dissolved, about 3 to 4 minutes. When cake is finished, let stand for 10 minutes, then turn out onto a cake plate or decorative platter. Pour syrup slowly over cake, letting it absorb. Decorate with lemon geranium leaves, and pile fresh berries in the center of the ring. Serve any extra syrup in a sauce boat to add as desired after the cake is sliced. Sometimes I double the sauce recipe just for this purpose. I use the same syrup, warm or cold, to pour over ripe berries to make an easy company dessert with a few sprigs of lemon mint.

INGREDIENTS

Cake

1 cup butter

1 cup sugar

3 large eggs, separated

1 cup sour cream

grated rinds of one lemon and one orange

$1^3/4$ cups all-purpose flour

1 teaspoon baking powder

1 teaspoon baking soda

Syrup

juice of 2 oranges

juice of 2 lemons

$1/2$ cup sugar

$1/2$ cup Grand Marnier or Cointreau

My Mike's Lemon Cheesecake

This recipe makes a large, rich cheesecake that can serve hordes of people; a sliver goes a long way. My family always favored this very lemony version. Use a springform pan 9 inches in diameter and 3^1/$_4$ inches high.

Make a graham cracker crust following the recipe on the package. You may need to double the quantities for so large a pan. Bake the crust and let cool. Reset the oven to 500 degrees.

INGREDIENTS

For the filling:

5 8-ounce packages of cream cheese

1^3/$_4$ cups sugar

3 tablespoons flour

^{1}/$_2$ teaspoon vanilla

grated rind of large lemon
  (avoid the white part)

^{1}/$_4$ cup milk

6 large eggs

Beat the cream cheese with the sugar. Add the flour, lemon rind, vanilla, and milk. Beat until smooth. Mix eggs lightly with a fork. Add to the cheese mixture, and slowly beat until blended. Pour slowly into graham cracker crust. Bake on middle rack in hot oven for 15 minutes. Then lower oven to 250 degrees and bake for 1 hour. If the cake seems to be browning too quickly on top as it bakes, place a piece of aluminum foil lightly over the top. Turn off oven and leave the door ajar until the cake completely cools, about 3 hours. Remove sides of pan, leaving cake on metal bottom.

For a special treat, place washed, hulled strawberries over the whole top of the cooled cake in concentric rings. Melt 1 cup currant jelly with 1 tablespoon water in the microwave or in a small pot on top of the stove. Then use a pastry brush to coat the strawberries with the glaze. Also dab some glaze on any little gaps between the berries. Pour any leftover jelly back into the jar and refrigerate for another use.

Lemon Cups

The surprise to this recipe is a delight to all; a layer of lemon sponge cake on top and a layer of lemon pudding on the bottom, produced with no extra work for the baker. Serving from one larger dish presents the portions in a less elegant way than with individual cups.

Preheat oven to 325 degrees. Beat egg whites until stiff but not dry. Beat butter and sugar together, then beat in flour, egg yolks, lemon juice, lemon rind, and milk. Fold in beaten egg whites. Pour into 4 individual ungreased custard cups or an 8-inch-diameter baking dish. Set in the oven in a shallow pan of water, and bake 35 minutes. Decorate the top with small lemon geranium leaves or other garnish. Serve warm or cool. Makes 4 servings.

INGREDIENTS

3/4 cup sugar

1 tablespoon butter

2 tablespoons all-purpose flour

2 eggs, separated

1 tablespoon finely grated lemon rind

1/4 cup lemon juice

1 cup milk, scalded and cooled

World's Best Lemon Squares

I have devoted a good part of my life to taste testing lemon bars—at covered-dish suppers, at PTA meetings, at country fairs, at auctions and craft shows, at bake sales, at the finest specialty food stores and bakeries in New York. Many are too sweet or don't have the proper balance of sweet to tart. Some, heaven forbid, are made with margarine instead of butter. Lemon bars are easy to pack for a picnic or in a lunch box, and if you eat only one you may console yourself that it is but a modest addition to your daily caloric intake.

Preheat oven to 350 degrees. Crumble the crust ingredients together with a pastry blender, a few quick pulses of a food processor, or your fingers. Press into bottom of lightly buttered 9-by-13-inch pan. Bake 20 minutes, until golden brown.

INGREDIENTS

Crust

two sticks butter, softened to room temperature

1/2 cup confectioner's sugar

2 cups all-purpose flour

Custard

4 large eggs, lightly beaten

1/2 cup lemon juice

1 1/2 cups granulated sugar

6 tablespoons flour

1 tablespoon lemon zest

Combine custard ingredients. Pour over baked crust. Bake until set, 20 to 25 minutes. Sprinkle with a light dusting of confectioner's sugar while still warm. Cut when cool. Makes 15 squares.

Also try these delicious variations: Add 1/2 cup miniature chocolate bits to the filling; the combination of citrus and chocolate is always a winner. Or, add 1/2 cup chopped pistachios to the crust and 2/3 cup whole pistachios to the filling.

Citrus Marmalade

A Welsh friend now lives in a community in Florida where all the plantings are communal property and a resident may gather fruit from a tree next to someone else's condo. When she's ready to make "real British marmalade," her husband goes out to gather what she needs. This recipe is totally different from that overly sweet, too finely cut American-style marmalade. Use organically grown fruit if possible, to avoid pesticides on the rinds.

INGREDIENTS

2 large lemons

2 navel oranges

2 ruby red grapefruits

granulated sugar

Wash fruit thoroughly. Cut, remove seeds, and chop into large pieces in a food processor. Measure chopped fruit. Pour into a big pot. Add three times the volume of water. Let stand for 12 hours or overnight, then boil for 20 minutes. Chop again in a food processor or blender, making the pieces as fine or as large as you like. Remeasure the fruit. For every cup of fruit, add 3/4 cup sugar. Bring to a boil and let boil rapidly, stirring until the temperature reaches 220 degrees on a candy thermometer. Pour into hot, sterilized canning jars or other lidded jars to refrigerate.

You can vary the proportions of the fruits to taste, keeping the ratios of water and sugar the same. You can also use the same recipe to make lemon-only marmalade. Homegrown 'Ponderosa' lemons make excellent marmalade.

Lemon Curd

Homemade lemon curd makes an ideal gift, if you can bear to part with a jar. My mother used to spread lemon curd on toast and, calling it "lemon pie," serve it for dessert. A dollop of lemon curd on a fruit plate makes an elegant treat for unexpected company. It's also a wonderful tea-time treat. Use organically grown lemons if possible, to avoid pesticides.

Beat eggs in a mixing bowl. Wash the lemons thoroughly. Grate the rind on the finest side of your grater, trying to include only the zest and not the white pith. Remove seeds and juice the lemons. Mix juice and rind in with the eggs and sugar. Cook the mixture in a double boiler on top of the stove,

INGREDIENTS

3 lemons

3 cups sugar

3 large eggs

4 tablespoons unsalted butter

Lemon curd fills a sponge roll with tangy flavor. Nasturtium flowers and lemon verbena leaves from the garden contribute contrasting color.

stirring constantly. The water must boil slowly, but don't allow the lemon curd to boil. Add the butter bit by bit as the mixture cooks, until it thickens. Pour into hot, sterilized jelly jars and seal. Or pour into ordinary jars and keep refrigerated up to a week. Makes about 3 cups.

If you try to cook this mixture in a saucepan without a double boiler, the eggs will scramble rather than thicken the lemon butter. To improvise a double boiler, stand a heatproof bowl inside a pan of slowly boiling water. The water should be well below the rim of the bowl so water won't spill over into the mixture. Check to be sure this all fits before you pour the lemon mixture into your invention.

This lemon butter is an excellent filling for any sponge jelly-roll recipe, including Passover sponge cakes. I frequently serve a lemon roll for a Thanksgiving dessert, as the combination of sponge cake and lemon seems light and refreshing after a heavy meal. Also use to fill prebaked tart shells, with or without sliced fresh fruit on top.

Lemon Balls

These are an excellent addition to your Christmas cookie repertoire. Children love to help roll the dough in their palms to form the balls.

INGREDIENTS

1 cup butter

$1/3$ cup confectioner's sugar

1 teaspoon vanilla

$3/4$ cup cornstarch

1 cup flour

1 tablespoon grated lemon rind

$1/2$ cup finely chopped pecans or walnuts

Cream butter and sugar together. Add vanilla and lemon rind. Add flour, cornstarch, and chopped nuts. Mix until the dough holds together. Cover and chill in the refrigerator for 1 hour or more, until you're ready to bake. Preheat oven to 375 degrees. Butter a cookie sheet. Form the dough into 1-inch balls and place on the cookie sheet. Bake for about 10 minutes, until lightly browned. Cool on a rack.

If desired, frost with icing made of 1 cup confectioner's sugar, 1 tablespoon soft butter, $1/2$ teaspoon finely grated lemon rind, and enough lemon juice to mix easily. Start with 1 tablespoon juice, and add more very gradually as needed to reach spreading consistency.

Easy Lemon Ice Cream

You can make this simple recipe even if you don't have an ice cream maker. It keeps in the freezer for about 2 weeks without becoming crystallized. I served this dessert at both of my sons' Bar Mitzvah luncheons at their request.

Mix juice, zest, and sugar, stirring well. Add cream and salt, stirring well again. Pour into freezing trays or a low bowl, and freeze until solid on the outside and mushy in the middle. Transfer to mixing bowl, and beat with electric mixer at medium speed for about 1 minute. Spoon into individual cups and refreeze. Before serving, remove from freezer and let stand 15 minutes to soften slightly. For special occasions, garnish with an edible flower, such as a pansy or nasturtium, a small sprig of mint, or a twist of lemon. Makes 8 servings

You can make individual serving cups out of real lemons. Stand the lemon on its tip and cut a 1/2-inch slice off one side. This will become the lid. Now set the lemon back on its side; the lemon container will look like a little boat. Scoop out all the flesh and as much of the white as possible, without cutting through the rind. Do the same on the lid. Save the flesh and juice for other purposes. Use these little lemon boats for the lemon ice cream or the strawberry mint sorbet, below, any other fruit ice cream, or any frozen soufflé. They freeze nicely.

INGREDIENTS

3 tablespoons lemon juice

2 teaspoons lemon zest

1 cup superfine sugar

2 cups light cream

1/8 teaspoon salt

Strawberry Mint Sorbet

Fill lemon boats described above with this refreshing pink confection. Individual servings make a more attractive presentation, and without the thawing and unthawing necessary to serve from a large bowl, you avoid crystallization.

Puree strawberries in a food processor with lemon juice and lemon mint or lemon balm leaves. Add sugar and water, and blend until smooth. Pour into ice cube trays or a

INGREDIENTS

1 1/2 cups fully ripe strawberries, washed and hulled

1 tablespoon chopped fresh lemon mint or lemon balm

juice of one lemon

3/4 cup sugar

1/4 cup water

shallow bowl. Allow to harden until edges are frozen solid but middle is still mushy. Scrape from freezer container and whip again in the food processor. Spoon into individual serving cups or lemon boats as in the lemon ice cream recipe and refreeze before serving. Makes 5 cups.

May Spector's Two-Crusted Lemon Pie

My sister and I never knew whether to beg our mother to make lemon meringue pie or this two-crusted lemon pie. Both delicious pies use the same crust recipe but a slightly different filling. Decide for yourself. The lemon meringue recipe follows.

Cut butter into flour with a pastry blender or a few pulses of a food processor. Add other ingredients, and blend until mixture just forms a ball. Divide dough in two balls, one slightly larger. Wrap in plastic wrap and refrigerate 3 hours or overnight. Then roll out on a floured board into two rounds. Make slits in the middle of the smaller one to let steam escape from the top while baking. Place the larger round in a 9-inch pie plate, edges draping over the sides. To make the filling, wash the lemon thoroughly. Grate the rind finely, avoiding the pith. Cut the lemon, remove the seeds, and extract the juice. Combine flour, sugar, and salt in a double boiler. Slowly stir in hot water. Add butter and cook, stirring until thickened. Cool slightly. Then stir in egg, juice, and lemon rind. Pour into pie crust. Place second pie crust over the top, and crimp edges. Cut off excess dough. With a pastry brush, brush the top of the pie crust with an egg yolk beaten with 1 tablespoon of water to make it shine. Bake in 400-degree oven for 10 minutes, then reduce heat to 350 degrees and let brown, about 20 minutes more. Don't cut until completely cool. (The top will be rather flat, but the taste divine.)

INGREDIENTS

Crust

$1/2$ cup unsalted butter

$1 1/2$ cups flour

1 tablespoon sour cream

1 tablespoon sugar

1 large egg yolk

1 tablespoon water

pinch of salt

$1/2$ teaspoon finely grated lemon zest

Filling

1 cup hot water

1 tablespoon flour

$1 1/4$ cups sugar

$1/4$ teaspoon salt

$1 1/2$ tablespoons butter

1 large lemon

1 egg, slightly beaten

1 egg yolk for glaze

May Spector's Lemon Meringue Pie

Note that the lemon filling in this recipe contains no cornstarch, tapioca, or arrowroot, all thickeners sometimes used to stabilize a custard. Mother believed that these additives, as well as agar or pectin in jellies and jams, were unnatural and made food impure. Besides, there was no need to provide more stability for her lemon fillings. The pie was gone in a flash on the rare occasions she baked it.

Use the same crust recipe as for the two-crusted lemon pie. Since this pie uses only a bottom crust, you can halve the recipe, but I prefer to make the whole thing and freeze the unused portion (up to a month) for my next pie. You can make the crust a day or two ahead or even keep it frozen, but the pie is best eaten the day you make it, as meringue slowly deflates over time.

Place pastry in ungreased 9-inch pie plate. Fold the edges under and crimp. Prick entire surface of dough, including the sides, with a fork to prevent shrinkage and warping of the bottom. Prebake the crust at 450 degrees for about 10 minutes. Let cool completely.

Preheat oven to 350 degrees.

To make the filling, separate the eggs and beat the yolks slightly. Place in top of double boiler with combined milk and water. Mix sugar, salt, and flour together. Add to egg mixture. Add zest, juice, and butter, and cook over boiling water, stirring frequently. With clean beaters, beat the egg whites until stiff but not dry. Slowly beat in ¹/₃ cup sugar until smooth and shiny and meringue forms stiff peaks when the beaters are raised. Pour custard into the prebaked crust. Completely cover custard to the edge of crust, sealing it with the egg white meringue. Swirl the meringue in fanciful puffs with a spoon as you pile it on. Bake for about 15 minutes, until the meringue is nicely browned. To get clean cuts, dip knife or pie server in hot water after each slice.

INGREDIENTS

Filling and Meringue

4 large eggs

1¹/₂ cups sugar

1 cup water

1 cup milk

4 tablespoons flour

juice of 3 lemons

finely grated zest of two lemons

1 tablespoon butter

pinch of salt

¹/₃ cup sugar for meringue

Lemon Sticks

The flower show in Rittenhouse Square, Philadelphia, was a highlight of spring when I was a girl. My mother always bought me a bunch of lily of the valley and a lemon stick to savor as I walked the paths of the outdoor show. The lemon stick man had a canopied cart, a supply of fresh lemons, and hard candy sticks. He cut a hole in one end of the lemon and inserted the candy stick. Then I would suck on the candy stick like a straw. At first nothing happened, but eventually the lemon juice began to funnel up through the candy stick into my mouth, producing a glorious sweet-sour combination. Sometimes at country fairs, I still see lemon sticks being offered for sale. They are a wonderful idea for a little girl tea or doll party. Give the children a selection of candy sticks to choose from.

INGREDIENTS

whole lemons

candy sticks in a variety of flavors, such as peppermint, lime, cherry, orange, or lemon

The Shaw girls taste their first lemon sticks—Joanna on the left, Madeleine on the right.

PHOTOS BY BARBARA SHAW

Poached Peaches

You can use either yellow or white peaches for this dessert. Substitute fully ripe, quartered Bartlett or Bosc pears when peach season is over. Skin peaches the easy way by submerging in a big bowl with boiling water for about a minute. Remove with a slotted spoon as you are ready to peel them. The skins should slip off easily.

Mix wine, sugar, lemon zest, and lemon juice in a stainless steel or enamel saucepan. Peel, halve, and pit the peaches, putting the halves in the mixture to keep from discoloring as you finish preparing each peach. Bring to a boil and simmer until soft, 10 minutes or more, depending on the ripeness of the peaches. Remove peaches from liquid with a slotted spoon into individual goblets. Remove and discard the herb leaves. Reduce the liquid to about a cup by boiling down. Allow to cool. Pour over peaches. Garnish with fresh herb leaves and a small cinnamon stick if desired. Makes 6 servings.

INGREDIENTS

6 large, ripe peaches

1¹/₂ cups red or white wine

¹/₃ cup sugar

zest of one lemon

¹/₄ cup lemon juice

¹/₂ cup chopped lemon geranium or lemon
  verbena leaves

Sources

Edible Landscaping
P.O. Box 77
Afton, VA 22920
800-537-3700
www.eat-it.com
Mail-order lemon trees and some herbs

Gardens Alive
5100 Schenley Place
Lawrenceburg, IN 47025
812-537-8650
www.gardens-alive.com
Natural pest-control products, such as moth lures and insecticidal soaps, catalog

Goodwin Creek Gardens
P.O. Box 83
Williams, OR 97544
541-846-7357
Herb plants and seeds, useful catalog

Logee's Greenhouses, Ltd.
141 North St.
Danielson, CT 06239-1939
888-330-8038
Lemon trees, scented geraniums, other lemon herbs

Meadow View Farm
371 Bowers Rd.
Kutztown, PA 19530
610-682-6094
Sells 175 varieties of hot peppers, including the 'Lemon Drop', 100 heirloom tomatoes, 30 eggplants, plants, fruits, pick-your-own, pepper jellies, ground peppers (no catalog)

LEFT: Container partners, lobelia 'Crystal Palace' and lemon mint.

Raintree Nursery
391 Butts Rd.
Morton, WA 98356
360-496-6400
www.raintreenursery.com
'Improved Meyer' lemon trees, as well
as other citrus, fruit trees and berries,
lemon grass, organic citrus food

Richters Seed Co.
Goodwin, ON L0C 1A0
Canada
905-640-6677
www.richters.com

Sandy Mush Herb Nursery
316 Surrett Cove Rd.
Leicester, NC 28748-5517
828-683-2014
A dozen lemon-scented geraniums and
other lemon herbs, herb plants and seeds,
interesting catalog

Shady Hill Gardens
821 Walnut St.
Batavia, IL 60510
Scented geranium plants, geranium
specialists, hundreds of other plants and
seeds (no catalog)

Territorial Seed Company
P.O. Box 157
Cottage Grove, OR 97424-0061
541-942-9547
www.territorial-seed.com
Nice selection of herb seeds

Well-Sweep Herb Farm
205 Mt. Bethel Rd.
Port Murray, NJ 07865
908-852-5390
Herb plants, potpourri supplies, books,
dried flowers, informative catalog

Further Reading

Becker, Jim, and Faye Brawner. *Scented Geraniums: Knowing, Growing, and Enjoying Scented Pelargoniums.* Loveland, CO: Interweave Press, 1996.

Black, Penny. *The Book of Potpourri.* New York, Simon & Schuster, 1989.

Duke, James A. *The Green Pharmacy.* Emmaus, PA: Rodale Press, 1997.

Klein, Maggie Blyth et al. *All About Citrus and Other Subtropical Fruit.* San Francisco: Orthor Books, 1985.

Kowalchik, Claire, and William Hylton, eds. *Rodale's Illustrated Encyclopedia of Herbs.* Emmaus, PA: Rodale Press, 1995.

PDR for Herbal Medicines. Montvale, NJ: Medical Economics Co., 1998.

Platt, Ellen Spector. *Lavender: How to Grow and Use the Fragrant Herb.* Mechanicsburg, PA: Stackpole Books, 1999.

———. *The Ultimate Wreath Book.* Emmaus, PA: Rodale Press, 1995.

Ray, Richard, and Lance Walheim. *Citrus: How to Select, Grow and Enjoy.* Tucson: HP Books, 1980.

Walheim, Lance. *Citrus: A Complete Guide to Selecting and Growing More Than 100 Varieties.* Ironwood Press, 1996.

Index